A Parent's Guide™ to

The Internet

by Ilene Raymond

parent's guide press

los angeles, california
www.pgpress.com

This book, and all titles in the *Parent's Guide* series, are available for purposes of fund raising and educational sales to charity drives, fund raisers, parent or teacher organizations, schools, government agencies and corporations at a discount for purchases of more than 10 copies. Persons or organizations wishing to inquire should call Mars Publishing at 1-800-549-6646 or write to us at **sales@marspub.com**.

Every effort has been made to bring you an error-free, informative book. If you find an error, or wish to simply comment to the author or publisher, please email us at **info@marspub.com**.

Dedication

To my three mice, experts in all things wired and weird: Jeff, Sasha and Noah.
Love and Kisses and Bunches of Thanks You's.

Edwin E. Steussy, CEO and Publisher
Lars W. Peterson, Editor
Michael P. Duggan, Graphic Designer

CONTENTS

Introduction

The Internet Ate My Kids!

Let's face it. As parents, many of us nurture a love/hate relationship when it comes to our kids and the Internet. I know I do. Gratifying as it is to observe my 9-year-old son researching the history of African rainsticks on the Web, watching him spend hours playing online games during a sunny afternoon sometimes makes me want to pitch the machine out the nearest window.

I'm not alone. Studies reveal that while most parents believe Internet access spells academic success, we're considerably less excited about other online activities like cruising the Web or downloading the latest 'N Sync lyrics.

Yet, as most parents will also admit, while the Internet can prove yet another distraction in a child's life already packed with television, video games and homework, not to mention gymnastics, piano lessons, religious school, and so on, it also can be an amazing tool for learning and fun.

No matter our trepidation, make no mistake about it: the Internet is here to stay. By the end of 2000, 44.4 million households were connected to the Internet, up from 12.7 million in 1995, an increase of nearly 250 percent over five years, according to the International Data Corporation (IDC). Thirty million children—or about 45 percent of all those under age 18—are now online. This figure is expected to reach 42 million by 2002, according to the Privacy Rights Clearinghouse. Three-quarters of kids currently in middle school and high school (ages 12-17) have access to the Internet, and 29 percent of those under 12 go online.

And although children still spend more time watching television than using computers, when a nationally representative sample of kids ages 8 to 18 were asked which medium they would rather carry to a desert island, more picked a computer with Internet access than any other medium, including television.

Despite kids' enthusiasm, relatively little research has been done on the effects of the Internet on children's development, mainly because the medium itself is still so new. However, most studies that have been conducted in the area of the Internet and kids have been encouraging. Keep in mind that research in this area is still in its infancy when reading these preliminary findings:

→ **Internet use may improve academic performance.** Kids and teens alike increasingly depend on the Internet for homework activities. Among teens aged 13 to 17, schoolwork surpassed games as the most frequent online activity according to a 1999 Annenberg study.

→ **Online games can improve cognitive skills.** Studies show that kids who play games often show improved visual intelligence skills—skills that may provide them with "training wheels" for computer literacy. By helping kids learn to manipulate images, games teach children skills useful in science and technology fields, where proficiency in manipulating images is increasingly important.

→ **The gender gap between boys' and girls' use of computers has narrowed.** Although boys aged eight to 13 continue to play more video and online games than girls, the gap vanishes when it comes to logging onto the Internet for chatting, visiting Web sites, using e-mail, doing schoolwork, or using the Internet to do a job. This held true for 14 to 18-year olds as well, except that older boys tend to visit more Web sites than older girls do.

→ **While much computer time is "spent alone," a majority of this time is spent communicating with others.** Much press attention has focussed on how Internet time robs kids of "real friendships." But it appears that a great deal of online time is spent connecting with others, particularly among teen girls. Romantic relationships between teens flourish online.

Clearly, more research is needed to see how the Internet impacts kids. So far, however, it appears safe to conclude that moderate use of the Internet can enhance kids' research skills and open new areas of communication. Using the Internet, kids can keep in touch not only with friends, but teachers, grandparents, and global pen pals.

More and more, the Internet will play a part in kids' education: whether that schooling takes place at home, in a classroom, at a community center, or a library. As an educational tool, kids will work collaboratively on projects that can put them in touch with experts around the world. Classrooms will be connected with each other, giving both teachers and students a chance to share information, observations, and problem solving techniques. Experts predict that these new technologies will change how children learn, altering forever the "top-down" model of a teacher dispensing information. In its place, new models of learning and teaching will emerge. Kids will embark on self-directed Web quests, move forward in the curriculum at a personally comfortable pace, and explore new options in how material is presented.

With unlimited information literally at their fingertips, the need for media literacy—the ability to examine and interpret knowledge critically—will be essential. The issue will no longer be how to gather information, but how to analyze material for its accuracy and reliability.

In addition, and perhaps most importantly, the Internet also offers kids another benefit: a chance to spend time with you. Younger kids will enjoy the chance to explore new Web sites and maybe make a site or two of their own with you as design or text consultant. Using streaming video and audio, you can watch animations, listen to live concerts, and chat with sports and entertainment celebrities. Teens, probably already proficient in the ways of the Web and beyond, can be cajoled into sharing their Net prowess with you in a refreshing (for them) role-reversal.

As a continually evolving medium, the Internet can be the perfect tool to build new family hobbies, develop fresh interests, and instill a love of lifelong learning in both parents and kids as they explore cyberspace—together.

About This Book

A Parents Guide to the Internet is based on my personal discovery of life online with my kids, supplemented by advice and opinions of educators, academics, and psychologists who study and explore the Internet for a living. As such, the book tries to dispense helpful tips on the nuts and bolts of Internet navigation, along with background on the birth of the Internet and its growing pains as it evolves: what place marketing plays online, how classrooms are adapting to new technology, how kids need to protect themselves (and we them) online.

But in addition, and perhaps most vitally, this is a handbook of projects and suggestions on how to become an Internet collaborator with your child.

Why is this so important? For a number of reasons. First of all, most of our kids speak, breathe and eat digital. If you want to know where your child travels on the Internet (the best way to protect them from heading to places you don't want them to go), you need to know the lingo. This doesn't mean becoming a geek or a programmer; it simply means learning to explore the Net, to join a chat room, and to master e-mail (at least to start).

Second, when you and your child go online together, you automatically set a great example. A Mom or Dad who shows a willingness to tackle new things—whether it's piano playing, Chinese cooking, or learning to program in C++ —brings an example of the 'life-long learner' into the household, without saying a word. Sure, you're going to make mistakes, but so what? You're in it for the long haul.

Third, working with your child online is fun. If the last time you remember creating something colorful was back in your own elementary school days, wait until you uncover a program like Paint Box and see how crayons and paints have grown up. Or, explore the delights of chatting with an expert on seashells or penguins or dinosaur bones. Sharing ongoing projects, like a family Web page or building a puzzle or playing a game, is not only a great way to bond, but a nice way to discover how two heads—or three or four, depending—are better than one.

Personally, I'm no Pollyanna when it comes to computers. I don't think the Internet is the answer to everything wrong with education, and I don't think that every site on the Internet is great for kids. But I am convinced of its great possibilities for adding to our—and our children's—experience of the world in a myriad of important ways. For example, I'm convinced that in the next decade, the Internet will usher in new ways of thinking and learning, not only for kids, but for all of us.

Many of these topics—working with your child, talking to them about values and safety online, teaching them by example—really have little to do specifically with the Internet. Instead, these ideas fall under the realm of good teaching and good parenting. Like any other activity you and your child share together— walking on the beach, learning to ride a bicycle, playing catch—you might find that in the process, you learn not only about riding a bike or seagulls or baseball, but a few tidbits about yourself and your child as well.

Call them bonus points.

How to Use This Book

Although most people refer to the "Internet" as though it were one single entity, in reality, there are many different ways to make use of Internet technology. Perhaps the most well known—and certainly the most popular—are applications that involve the World Wide Web. Along with the Web comes e-mail, chat and discussion boards, Instant Messaging, audio and video applications, and other multimedia uses. The first half of the guide offers an introduction to what you can do online, while the second covers parenting issues affected by the Internet.

Chapter 1: What is the Internet, anyway? – This chapter will give you a quick overview of the history of the Internet—its early beginning to how it has evolved today. You'll find thumbnail sketches of some of the most important figures in Internet history as well as a clear explanation of what the Internet is.

Chapter 2: Searching for Luther – As the most widely used element of the Internet, the Web's sheer volume of offerings can be daunting to a newcomer. Here you'll find a description of the Web, an explanation of a Web 'address,' and a real-life search for Luther Burbank, during which my son Noah and I explore a variety of Web search sites, many specifically designed for children. You'll also find answers to some of the Web's most pressing questions, like the difference between a search engine and a directory and when to use one and not the other.

Chapter 3: Sending E-mail – The second most common use of the Internet, e-mail is explained and explored in this chapter. Along with an easy-to-use guide to sending and receiving e-mail, we'll look at fun projects to do with your child, such as finding a keypal, joining a listserv, and how to contact the President.

Chapter 4: Chatting and Discussion Boards – Although chatting remains a popular feature of the Internet, many chat rooms are definitely not rated 'G' or 'PG.' To combat this problem, this chapter explores the mechanics of IRC chat and Instant Messaging, and then presents a number of child-friendly areas that are monitored for intruders and inappropriate language or activities. The second half covers Discussion Boards, where kids and parents can post messages and trade information about everything from sports to arts and crafts.

Chapter 5: Building a Web Page – The ultimate art project, Web pages offer kids and parents a chance to write, draw, and design, all the while teaching valuable computer skills. Whether you use a "What You See Is What You Get" or "WYSIWYG" editor or Hypertext Markup Language, this chapter is a great primer for learning the ins and outs of how to build a basic Web site.

Chapter 6: Playing Around – Games—single and multiplayer—draw many kids, teens and adults to the Internet. In this chapter we'll discuss how games can affect kids' behavior, tips on how to balance your kids' online time with other activities, and where to find non-violent, age-appropriate games online.

Chapter 7: Classroom, Home schooling and Distance Learning   With most American schools linked to the Internet, the next ten years will see profound changes in how technology is used in American schooling. We explore ways the Internet will impact education, how the Internet has contributed to the rise of home schooling, and how to evaluate the many long-distance courses available online for grades K-12 and beyond.

Chapter 8: Teens Online – As the generation who has grown up with the Internet, teens have adapted to and adopted the Internet for their own social, educational, and political uses. Here you'll find everything you want to know about IM chat, peer-to-peer music trading, streaming audio and video and teen e-commerce is here, along with recent surveys on how teens spend their online time.

Chapter 9: Selling It! – Plenty of sites and games on the Internet are free—or are they? With the Internet so popular with teens and kids, marketers—scrupulous and otherwise—see a prime target audience, ready to buy their products. A discussion of why Web advertising is different than other forms of media, privacy issues for the under-13 set, and what your kid should know before clicking that banner ad.

Chapter 10: Protecting Kids Online – You've read the media tales of child predators and pornographic, violent, and hate-filled online sites, but how dangerous is the Web? While the dangers may have been exaggerated, protecting your kids from strangers and uncomfortable areas of the Web can be as simple as designing a joint family policy with a few simple safety rules. We have examples of both.

Chapter 11: Content Filtering – Information about the latest technologies designed to filter Web content including content filters and filtered Internet Service Providers.

Chapter 12: What's Next? – Where will kids and the Internet be headed in the next ten or twenty years? Here you'll find some predictions from educators, psychologists, and other experts.

Happy traveling!

Want a Web License?

PBS Kids...http://pbskids.org/did_you_know/license
Young children can take a test to get their Web License (suitable for driving on the information highway, hem). If you're new to the Net (a 'newbie'), you and your child might want to take it together to see if your Web know-how measures up.

What is the Internet, Anyway?

Chapter 1

What Is the Internet, Anyway?

My son, at the tender age of 9, often helps his third grade teacher with a balky class-room computer. A fact of life: by age 8, most kids know their way around a mouse pad better than many adults do. Yet despite his skill, my son shows zero interest in employing the Internet for anything as practical as, say, homework. Heading online means e-mailing his baseball buddies with the team's latest stats or playing virtual golf. Suggestions on turning to the Net for knowledge do not compute.

What finally cracked Noah's resistance, however, was a bit of parental sub-terfuge. Rather than urging him yet again to use the Web to research a homework project, I offered a dare. Did he know where the Internet came from?

A shrug. "The computer, Mom."

"Yes, but, who made up the Internet?"

A roll of the eyes. "Everyone knows that. Bill Gates."

I shook my head and played my trump card. "No. But your brother knows the answer."

He looked up, snagged. Knowing everything his 16-year-old brother knows is Noah's quest, his private Holy Grail.

"Fine," he said.

Victory.

Want More?

Detailed information about the times and lives of scientists behind the Internet can be found—naturally—online.

The granddaddy of timelines, the Hobbes' Time Line highlights key events and technologies which helped shape the Internet as we know it today, as well as providing graphs and charts documenting the changes. Links take you to some of the original doc-uments behind the development of the Internet. Find it at: **ww.zakon.org. robert/internet/timeline.**

A detailed biography and reference site on WWW inventor, Tim Berners-Lee, can be found at **http://www.ideafinder.com/history/inventors/berners-lee.htm**. For his official site, at the World Wide Web Consortium (the organization that sets protocols and standards for use and design of the Web) see **www.w3.org/people/burners-lee/overview.html**. Also, see his book, *Weaving the Web*.

The Internet Society (ISOC) site covers the history of the Internet in depth, narrated at some points by the original thinkers, scientists, and developers. See **www.isoc.org/ internet**. For a comprehensive site that includes timelines on the development of the Net, plus capsule biographies and photos of the behind-the-scene scientists and designers, go to **www.pbs.org/opb/nerds2.0.1**

Nothing but Net

To begin: Where did the Internet come from? And if Bill Gates didn't invent it, who did?

The correct answer to the first question is a great many people. Some early visionaries include Vannevar Bush, a pioneer in the development of radar, who in 1945 wrote an article about a photo-electrical-mechanical device called a "Memex" (for memory extension) that might make and follow links between documents on microfiche—a precursor of the modern Web. (You can find his article on the *Atlantic Magazine* Web site.) Another is Doug Engelbart, who in the early 1960s designed the NLS "oN Line System" using hypertext browsing that links information together with a click of the mouse. NLS also included e-mail and word processing. (Along the way, Englebart also invented the mouse.)

The foundation for our modern Internet goes back to 1958. Following the launch of the Russian Sputnik, the first Earth-orbiting satellite, President Dwight D. Eisenhower created the Advanced Research Project Agency (ARPA) to oversee space and military programs, along with new computer and communication programs.

The Internet began in the late 1960s as ARPA scientists started to connect university and government computers. Scientists and researchers needed to exchange data and electronic mail, while Defense Department officials wanted to use the new networked computers to communicate if a nuclear war caused conventional communications technologies to collapse. For twenty years, Internet use was limited to these small groups of intelligence and military specialists.

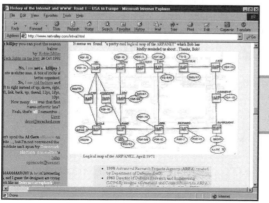

A 'logical map' of the ARPANET, April 1971.

Then, in 1989, Tim Berners-Lee, a British researcher at the European Laboratory for Particle Physics (CERN) outside Geneva, created a system that would make it easier for scientists to use the Internet to share information. Berners-Lee defined the core elements of the Web—a text formatting system (Hypertext Markup Language or HTML), a communications standard (Hypertext Transfer Protocol or HTTP), and an addressing scheme to locate Web sites (Uniform Resource Locators or URLs). Then he built a rudimentary browser.

The man behind the World Wide Web: Tim Berners-Lee.

In 1993, a handful of students working for the National Center for Supercomputing Applications (NCSA) at the University of Illinois took Berners-Lee's invention, integrated graphics and multimedia features into the browser, and made it run on mass-market computing platforms, such as Windows and the Macintosh. The result was Mosaic. Most of the browsers available today, including Netscape's Navigator and Microsoft's Internet Explorer, have descended in some way from NCSA's Mosaic.

Mosaic launched a wave of innovation that led, in turn, to an ever-expanding technological alphabet soup. People working with the Internet have had to learn new concepts and new vocabularies almost daily. In addition to HTTP and HTML, other early standards that defined how the Internet could send and receive information were FTP (File Transfer Protocol) along with the fundamental TCP/IP (Transmission Control Protocol/Internet Protocol), which is the basic packaging (the TCP part) and address scheme (the IP part) of data and computers on the Internet. Many other standards quickly emerged for sending data and even video pictures and telephone conversations across the Internet.

Not only has the technology been moving fast (and faster) ever since, but the number of Internet users has multiplied every year. In 1993, the primary users of the Internet were scientists, professors, and engineers at university and government labs and a handful of corporations. By 1999, there were 200 million users around the globe. Web commerce also exploded from zero in 1993 to $22 billion in 1998, with predictions of hundreds of billions of dollars to be spent in the twenty-first century.

An Internet Timeline

The 1960's

1960 –

J.C.R. Licklider, a Massachusetts Institute of Technology researcher, publishes a paper describing how men and computers might cooperate to solve problems.

1962 –

Paul Baran, a Rand Corporation scientist working for the ARPA, designs a computer network model on paper.

1965 –

Work begins on the Advanced Research Project Agency network (ARPAnet), a network intended to promote the sharing of information between super-computers used by U.S. researchers.

1967 –

Larry Roberts, a computer scientist at ARPA, proposes a design for a fast decentralized network built on telephone lines.

1968 –

First generation of networking hardware and software designed. The contract to build the Interface Message Processors (IMPS) at the core of the developing ARPA network is given to Bolt, Beranek, and Newman (BBN), a technical consulting firm in Cambridge, Massachusetts.

1969 –

The first four ARPA network hosts located at Stanford Research Institute, UCLA, UC Santa Barbara, and the University of Utah are connected, permitting users of one research computer to "talk to" another university's computer. CompuServe begins as a computer time-sharing service.

The 1970's

1970 –

ALOHAnet, a network designed by Norm Abramson, a professor of engineering, starts up at the University of Hawaii. Eventually, it will be hooked up to the ARPAnet.

1972 –

Ray Tomlinson, a BBN engineer, writes one of the first e-mail programs, and establishes the use of the @ sign. Later that year, programs are created to list, forward, and reply to messages. E-mail quickly becomes the most popular application of the Internet, serving as a high-speed digital post office for people to collaborate on projects and discuss topics online.

1974 –

Vint Cerf and Bob Kahn publish a paper that describes the Transmission Control Protocol (TCP) to improve the efficiency of the network and allow different networks to connect together into one big network—an Internet. ARPAnet goes global, with connections to the University College, London, England and the Royal Radar Establishment in Norway.

1974-1981 –

The general public gets its first hints on how networked computers can be used in daily life when the commercial version of the ARPAnet (BNN's Telenet) goes online, and the network begins to move away from its original military/research roots.

1975 –

Microsoft is founded by Bill Gates and Paul Allen to produce software for microcomputers.

1979 –

Tom Trustcott and Jim Ellis, grad students at Duke University, and Steve Bellovin at the University of North Carolina develop USENET, which allows users from all over the world can join discussion groups to talk about the Net, politics, and thousands of other subjects.

The 1980's

1981 –

IBM launches the first personal computer (PC), forever changing the computer landscape.

1982 –

The term 'Internet' is used for the first time.

1982-87 –

Bob Kahn and Vint Cerf are key members of a team that develops TCP/IP, the common language of all Internet computers.

1988 –

Robert Morris, a computer science graduate at Cornell University, releases a malicious program called the "Internet Worm" that brings down 6,000 hosts, or ten percent of all the machines on the network. The "hacker" arrives.

1989 –

Over 100,000 hosts are now connected to what is popularly called the Internet.

A Recipe for Access

To get online, you'll need one of each of the ingredients listed below.

→   A computer.

→   A Web browser. A browser is software that lets you look at the different resources on the Internet. Two of the most popular are Netscape Navigator and Microsoft Explorer.

→   A modem. A modem transforms digital signals from your computer (bits of binary information) into analog signals (traditional electronic frequencies used in telephones and televisions) so information can travel through your telephone wires. On the return trip, the modem converts analog signals back to digital.

→   A regular voice telephone line.

→   An Internet Service Provider (ISP). The ISP provides services to access the Internet and other related services such as Web site hosting. To find an ISP consult **www.thelist.internet.com** or **www.thedirectory.org**.

The 1990's

1990 –

ARPAnet ceases to exist.

1991 –

The World Wide Web arrives when Tim Berners-Lee posts the first public Web software on the alt.hyperext.newsgroup. Called Enquire, short for 'enquire within upon everything', a phrase from a Victorian-era encyclopedia he recalled from boyhood, this software would, as he put it, keep "track of all the random associations one comes across in real life and brains are supposed to be so good at remembering but sometimes mine wouldn't." Enquire links these ideas together. Words could be linked to files in his computer, and eventually other peoples' computers—an idea that eventually spawned the World Wide Web. He also put together a primitive browser program that permitted words, pictures, and sounds to appear on screen using technology no more difficult than word processing.

1992 –

The number of Internet hosts surpasses one million.

1993 –

Marc Andreeson and a group of student programmers at NCSA (National Center for Supercomputing Applications located at the University of Illinois at Urbana Champaign) develop and release a graphical browser for the World Wide Web called Mosaic.

1994 –

Marc Andreeson and Jim Clark start Netscape. Pizza Hut begins taking orders over the Internet. The Rolling Stones Voodoo Lounge tour is broadcast online.

1995 –

The Web dominates Internet traffic. The first version of streaming video appears. CompuServe and AOL provide dial-up access to the Internet for the first time. Digital launches its AltaVista search engine, the first serious attempt to index the Web. Jeff Bezos opens the online bookstore, Amazon.com. E-bay accepts its first bids.

Microsoft releases Windows 95, along with the company's first Web browser, Internet Explorer.

1996 –

Nearly ten million hosts are now online, with 40 million people online around the globe. Browser wars begin heating up as Microsoft and Netscape both release the third version of their browsers.

1999 –

The number of Internet users passes 200 million...

Speed Rules

Forget the turtle and the hare: when it comes to modems, go for speed.

Faster modems mean a zippier Internet. This is because the quicker the modem, the greater the bandwidth (the amount of information flowing from the Internet in a given time).

The amount of information modems can carry is measured in kilobits per second (KBPS). Although older modems once transferred information in 14.4 KBPS and 28.8 KBPS, since 1998 most new computers come equipped with 56 KBPS modems.

And, If you decide to use an Integrated Digital Network adapter in place of a modem, the bandwidth can rise to 128 KBPS. Digital Subscriber Line systems (DSL) and Cable modems can boost speeds to mega-bit range.

Did You Know?

In 1866, long before the beginning of the Internet, Queen Victoria and President Andrew Johnson exchanged messages across the first fully functional telegraph cable across the Atlantic. Over a hundred years later, in 1976, Queen Elizabeth II sent the first royal e-mail from the Royal Signals and Radar Establishment in the U.K.

And Now?

Today's Internet is a worldwide "network of networks" that allows all types of computers to communicate and share services. Thousands of computers make up the network itself, while millions more are connected to the networks.

No one group is in charge of the Internet. Organizations that develop technical aspects of the network and set standards or develop new applications of the technology exist, but no 'governing' body is in control.

The modern Internet offers a wide variety of services: electronic mail, file transfer, vast information resources, interest group membership, interactive collaboration, multimedia displays, real-time broadcasting, shopping opportunities, breaking news, and much more. Electronic mail (e-mail) has replaced Post Office 'snail mail' for many users. Internet Relay Chat (IRC) permits you to have live "conversations" with other users, while telephony hardware and software offer real-time voice conversations, much like using the telephone.

As mentioned above, the most explosive growth on the Internet is the World Wide Web (WWW or simply, the Web). Using hypertext, a method of instant cross-referencing, you can travel from one piece of information to another with a single mouse click. Your Web browser can bring you into contact with literally millions of pages on the Web, and millions of people around the world.

"So that's pretty much it," I tell Noah. "Any questions?"

"Yeah," he says. "What about that guy?"

"What guy?"

"You know that Al Gore guy who said he invented the Internet. Where does he fit in?"

"Ask your brother," I sigh.

Interplanetary Internet

While colonies on Mars or Jupiter may be years in the works, scientists are already planning on e-mail between various surface landers and orbiting satellites. Additional internets could appear elsewhere, all linked to form a huge Interplanetary Internet.

Researcher Vincent Cerf, an Internet founding father, is adviser to the space project. The project has received $500,000 from the U.S. Defense Advanced Research Projects Agency, the same group that first funded the Internet.

How do computers talk to one another?

One of the original goals of the Internet was to let computers "talk" to one another. And even though the Net has expanded many, many times since that first notion, the basic concept of computers 'talking' to one another remains.

As with any other forms of communication, to understand one another, they need to speak the same language. In this case, that language is Transmission Control Protocol/Internet Protocol (TCP/IP). No matter what they're up to—videoconferencing, bringing you pictures on the Web, or sending e-mail—computers use TCP/IP.

When you get down to it, however, TCP/IP is less an actual tongue and more of an agreement about how computers share information. Because most users have agreed to use the protocol, it has become the standard. Agreeing to use TCP/IP means that:

→ Each computer on the network has its own Internet Protocol address, even yours when you dial up to check e-mail. (Though your IP, assigned to you by your Internet Service Provider, probably changes each time you log on).

→ Information files will be sent to and from these addresses. To accomplish this, a file is broken into smaller pieces, called packets, that contain information about their ultimate destination, and how they fit in with the rest of the packets to make the file. The packets are put back together when they reach their destination. This is the Transfer Control Protocol.

→ A valuable side-effect of this method is that packets can follow different routes in their travels, so that if one route is blocked, they can take an alternate pathway.

Collaborators in Invention

Although we tend to link a single inventor per invention, the truth is often more complicated and interesting. Some other inventions and inventors to explore on the Web:

Samuel Morse made a number of improvements to the telegraph, a machine already developed in Germany. Always a good "idea" man, he lacked engineering skills to carry his plans through, so he often turned to others for help. As for the Morse code, despite carrying Sam's last name, Alfred Vail wrote it. For more, see **http://web.mit.edu/invent/www/inventorsI-Q/morse.html**.

On March 10, 1876, in Boston, Massachusetts, Alexander Graham Bell invented the telephone. Thomas Watson fashioned the device from a wooden stand, a funnel, a cup of acid, and some copper wire. With these simple parts, and a simple first message—"Mr. Watson, come here, I want you!"—he completed the first telephone call and filed for a patent only hours before his competitor, Elisha Gray. Learn more at **www.privateline.com/TelephoneHistory/History1.htm**.

While Vladimir Kosma Zworkykin, a Russian-born American inventor, is often credited with inventing television, the image his set displayed was no more than one inch high. Philo Taylor Farnsworth, who immersed himself in research on television picture transmission, was the first to transmit a television image comprised of 60 horizontal lines. (The first image? A dollar sign.) Future inventors like Peter Goldmark of CBS later revolutionized the medium with his three-filter system allowing color. Read all about it at **www.inventorsmuseum.com/television.htm**.

Searching The
World
Wide Web

Chapter 2

Searching the World Wide Web

You can't escape it. Whether you go to the supermarket, a book store or train station, you may have noticed that that almost everything is in the grip of the Web. Web addresses—those mysterious WWW.com's—have sprung up across the nation, adorning billboards, magazines, and advertisements for everything from mascara to cat food. The Web is the primary reason why so many people have gotten online. In this chapter, you'll pick up some basic vocabulary of the Web, along with tips for searching and travelling online.

We're Only Browsing

Although most folks use the terms Internet and World Wide Web interchangeably, they really are two different creatures. The Internet is a "network of networked computers" which permits thousands upon thousands of machines around the world to exchange all kinds of digital files—text, video, audio. The Web, on the other hand, is but the most popular use of the Internet—the text, graphic images, sound, video, and other multimedia resources in a convenient package.

Technically, the Web covers all resources on the Internet that use the Hypertext Transfer Protocol (HTTP). HTTP is the set of rules for exchanging files (text, graphic images, sound, video, and other multimedia files) on the Web. The main thing you need to know about HTTP is that it permits you to click onto a link—usually a differently colored or underlined word or phrase in a document—and be immediately transferred from one page to another.

All WWW pages are formatted using Hypertext Markup Language (HTML). Other features may be added to Web pages using special tools, such as Java, a programming language that operates independently of your computer's operating system. Java "applets"—little programs added to your Web browser—let you add animation or greater interactivity, like chat, or animation, to HTML documents. (For more on HTML and how to build a Web page, see Building Your Own Web Page, Chapter 5.)

Millions upon millions of pages fill the Web. But even if you know where you want to head, how does your computer know where to go? Why doesn't it get lost in all those files?

The simple answer lies in your trusty browser program. Browsers fetch Web pages from other computers on the network. They are also configured to run audio and visual programs; perform secure e-commerce transactions; run Java applets; filter Internet sites based on ratings systems, as well as to perform other sophisticated uses. The two most popular browser programs are Microsoft Internet Explorer and Netscape Navigator.

Basically, a browser works as follows: When you ask to open a Web file by either typing in the Web address or clicking on a hypertext link, your browser program files an HTTP request with the Web server on a remote computer. An HTTP 'daemon' program designed to wait for such requests and handle them when they arrive takes your request, processes the information, and then sends the desired page back to the client, your computer, and—voilà—the page pops up on your screen.

Search Engines:

Alta Vista	**www.altavista.com**
Go	**www.go.com**
Google (an excellent choice)	**www.google.com**
HotBot	**www.hotbot.com**
Lycos	**www.lycos.com**
Northern Light	**www.northernlight.com**
Planet Search	**www.planetsearch.com**

Directories:

Yahoo!	**www.yahoo.com**
Excite	**www.excite.com**
DMOZ	**www.dmoz.com**
Librarians Index to the Internet	**www.lii.org**
Look Smart.com	**www.looksmart.com**
NBCi	**www.nbci.com**
Select Surf	**www.selectsurf.com**
Study Web	**www.studyweb.com**

What's That Address?

To find that page, the browser needs either a click on a hyperlink or a specific address or (in tech speak) a Uniform Resource Locator (URL). A URL is the address of a file (or resource) accessible on the Internet. The type of resource depends on the Internet application protocol. Addresses beginning with 'HTTP://' signal that the resource can be found on the Web.

The URL contains the name of the protocol required to access the resource, a domain name that identifies a specific computer on the Internet, and a description of a file location on that computer.

Let's break down a fictitious, though delicious address.

http://www.tonyspizza.com/anchovies.html

→ **http:** This describes a resource to be accessed with an HTTP (Web browser) application.

→ **www.tonyspizza.com:** The name of the computer where the resource is located.

→ **anchovies:** The specific file we're after.

→ **html:** Hypertext Markup Language (HTML) describes to the browser how the page will be displayed on your monitor. (More on HTML, what it is and how to use it, can be found in Chapter 5.)

The first page you see when you open your Web browser is your home page. If you look on the tool bar, you'll see a slot for "address," next to which you'll find the address of your home page, which in this case is **www.msn.com**.

Home page for Microsoft Internet Explorer browser.

Keep your eye on this spot (located right under the toolbar). Every time you move to another site, the new URL will appear.

Let's give your browser a test run. Click the mouse once to clear the space, and then type in the Web address to your destination: **www. lawrencegoetz.com/ programs/mousepractice**. Press enter and—presto chango—you should be sent to that site.

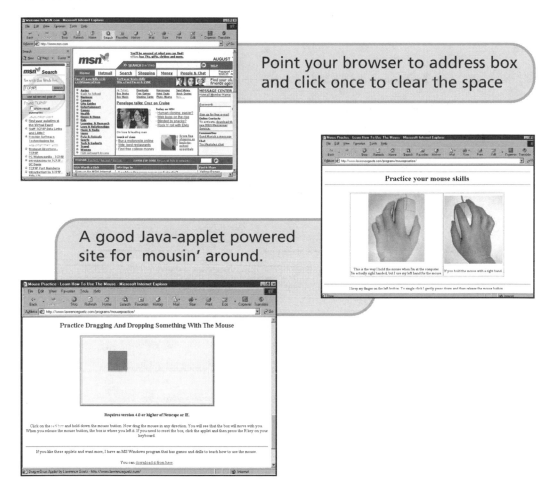

Point your browser to address box and click once to clear the space

Practice your mouse skills

A good Java-applet powered site for mousin' around.

Practice Dragging And Dropping Something With The Mouse

Search Sites

Having mastered your browser, you're ready to rule the Web. All you need is to click on a link or plug in a URL.

But what if you know what you want to find, but you don't have the address? Don't panic: it's a dilemma shared by all users. With millions upon millions of Web pages to choose from, there's no way to keep track of all those URLs in your head. Recognizing this problem, a number of companies have developed search sites to help: search engines and directories.

What is a Search Engine?

Search engines have three parts:

1. *A "spider" (also called a "crawler" or a "bot"). A spider travels around the Web to collect addresses, page titles, key words, and brief descriptions described in HTML 'Metatags' that appear on individual Web sites.*

2. *A program to catalog this information. Web page descriptions and addresses brought back by the spider are gathered in a huge index or 'catalog' that serves as the database for the search engine.*

3. *A program that retrieves database information. Upon entering a keyword or phrase in the search engine, this program searches for your request, then returns the results to you in a list of likely 'hits'—sites that contain (hopefully) the information you seek.*

Both Netscape Navigator and Microsoft Internet Explorer offer search engines that you can use from your browser home page. Neither, however, can compare in scope or power to some other commercial engines around the Web. To get to another search site, simply type the URL (such as Google, **www.google.com**) in the address box. Or search for a search engine on your browser site, and click on the link.

Employing a search engine is easy. Locate the space marked "search." Then enter what you're looking for. For some engines, this can be done in "natural language," for example, "What is an elephant?" For others, you can simply enter a phrase or keywords, such as "Asian Elephants."

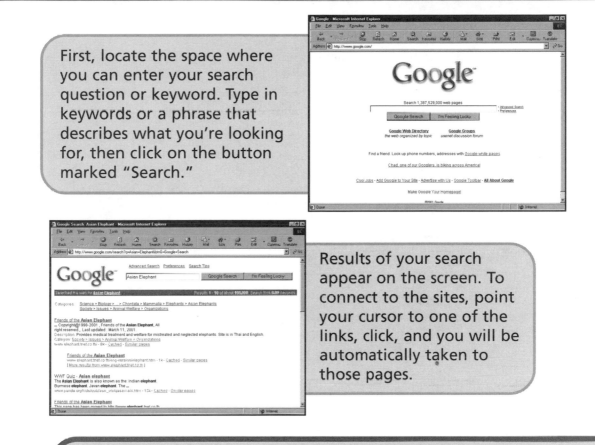

First, locate the space where you can enter your search question or keyword. Type in keywords or a phrase that describes what you're looking for, then click on the button marked "Search."

Results of your search appear on the screen. To connect to the sites, point your cursor to one of the links, click, and you will be automatically taken to those pages.

Metasearch engines

(sites that run a search of several search sites at the same time):

All-in-one-Search Page	**www.allonesearch.com**
CNET Search	**www.search.com**
Dogpile (we've had lots of luck here)	**www.dogpile.com**
Ixquick	**www.iquick.com**
Ithaki	**www.ithaki.net/kids**
Metacrawler	**www.metacrawler.com**
Momma	**www.momma.com**
ProFusion	**www.profusion.com**
The Big Hub	**www.thebighub.com**
Web Crawler	**www.webcrawler.com**

Directories

A directory can be another handy way of finding information, particularly if you're new to the Web or aren't quite sure what you're searching for. Directories link pages together by categories, moving from major topics to subtopics. Probably the best known directory is Yahoo! (**www.yahoo.com**).

Because directory subjects are linked, however, you can easily get off the subject. But you might also discover some pages you'd never have thought of. At the top of the home page, you'll see your browser's toolbar, where you'll find the address of the page currently appearing on your computer screen. Each time you switch pages, the new address location will appear in that same spot.

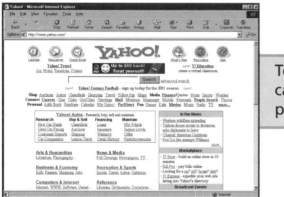

To start, we clicked on a category from the main page, animals.

At the Animals site, we narrowed our search to Mammals, then clicked onto elephants.

Whether you choose to use a directory or a search engine, be aware that large search engines and directories cover the entire Web, unlike smaller, more specialized search engines that may only cover selected parts of the Web. For parents who wish to protect their kids from inappropriate material, you may want to restrict searches to kids' Webs or specialized Web areas, many of which will be described below.

Also, as you'll learn when you post your own Web page to search engines, the first entries that pop up don't always mean that they're the best entries: only that they contain most specifically (to the search engine's satisfaction) the answer to your specific request. In other words, the keywords you entered best matched the keywords the Web site designer 'advertised' on his site with 'Metatags.' Therefore, if you don't get what you want on your first try, you can either refine your search (we'll tell you how) or switch to a different search engine or directory.

The independence and diversity of the Web means you don't have to take what you get; it can reward a persistent, focused searcher.

Find the link for 'elephants,' click, and you'll be linked to a number of sites featuring elephant info.

The Challenge: Locate Luther

It started with watermelon. Our family was sitting around the dinner table, eating the first fresh watermelon of the season. All of us agreed that it wasn't the greatest watermelon we'd ever eaten. Noah claimed to know why.

"No seeds."

"Really?"

My oldest son nodded. "I think he's right."

I didn't know if seeds were or were not to blame. So I did what I usually do when I don't know the answer: change the subject.

"Ever hear of Luther Burbank?" I asked Noah.

Watermelon juice seeped down his chin.

"Well," I began, in this awful studious way I have when I want to 'impart wisdom.' "He was a botanist. He," I looked to my husband Jeff for support, but he looked the other way. "spliced together trees."

"Watermelon doesn't grow on trees."

"Look," I said. "Maybe we could investigate Luther Burbank." My enthusiasm heightened. "Pin down this watermelon thing."

Noah took another bite of watermelon; I took it for a 'yes.'

So began our search for Luther.

And We're Off...

Looking for Luther is one thing; finding him online is another. We know he's out there—the question is where? Part of the problem—for everyone on the Net—is the sheer volume of Web sites. According to KidsClick!, in March 1999, the number of Web sites went over 4,389,000. Another guess said that by Spring 1999, there were 800 million Web pages. As I write this in August 2001, no one I've consulted seems willing to make a guess.

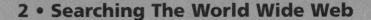
Encyclopedias

Noah and I started our search for Luther Burbank with the old friend of teachers and schoolchildren everywhere, the encyclopedia. We first headed for Encyclopedia.com from the Electric Library (**www.encyclopedia.com**) one of several encyclopedia search sites online. Others include Encarta (**www.encarta.com**), The Columbia Encyclopedia (**www.bartleby.com/65/**), and Britannica.com (**www.britannica.com**). All feature short articles on a variety of topics.

Organized alphabetically, the online digitized Encyclopedia.com works in two ways: by keyword or by clicking on the pictured alphabetized spine.

Using the search feature, we entered Luther Burbank's name and clicked the search button—a familiar method of searching. But alternately, **www.encyclopedia.com** has a cool tool that lets you simply click on any of the alphabeticized spines of the volume's pictured on the home page. A click on 'B' whisks us to a listing of topics starting with that letter. Using the mouse, we can scan the selections until we located 'Burbank, Luther.'

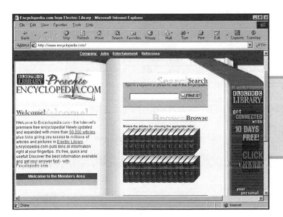

To find Luther Burbank; click the B volume of the encyclopedia spine.

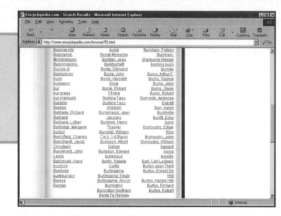

This brings up a long list of subjects starting with the letter B. We use our crack alphabetical skills to find Mr. Burbank.

For comparison's sake, we decided to try out Luther on a different encyclopedia site to compare information and headed for **www.britannica.com**. Noah typed in "luther burbank" (even though he does know that proper names begin with caps), and hit the search button, which led us (despite his lower case letters) to our man (and a snide request that asked if we really *meant* to spell his name correctly).

In addition to a larger biography, you'll notice that this site also did a preliminary search of the Web for us, and found an interesting site devoted to Mr. Burbank. Plus, the site offered to link us to other articles dealing with his work in plants and genetics in history and agriculture. While this may have been a little more than a nine-year-old needed to know, a teen working on a research paper might find those links useful.

Sorry, Wrong Address

Weaving around the Web, you can't avoid it: the dreaded "404 not found" or "Not found on this server" message. What should you do?

→ Check your spelling. Web addresses can get complicated.

→ Scan your capitals. When it comes to capital or lower case letters, Web sites are exact.

→ Head for a search engine. Fluidity, thy name is Web. Don't worry if the name of the site you're looking for has changed; chances are good that the old site has simply changed names and reconfigured at a new location. Run a search of the topic of the old site to see if it pops up.

→ Work with some variations. Play with the old name and see if you can find the new location. If the original site was **www.muggle.com**, try **www.muggles.com** or **www.themuggles.com**. You might get lucky.

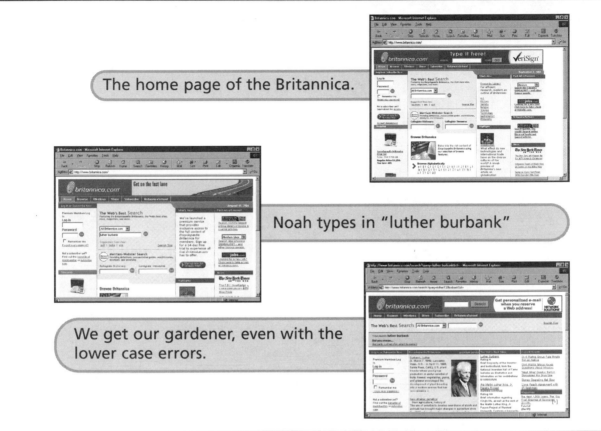

The home page of the Britannica.

Noah types in "luther burbank"

We get our gardener, even with the lower case errors.

Common top-level domain names

You've seen them, you love them, but do you know what they mean? Evaluating pages on the Web—where they come from and if they present certain points of view—can start by noting the top-level domain.

.com	**Commercial enterprises**
.edu	**Educational institutions or universities**
.org	**Non-commercial organizations**
.gov	**United States government agency**
.mil	**United States military organization**
.net	**Network, such as Internet service providers**
.ca	**Canada**
.uk	**United Kingdom**

A, B, C's...

Since we're in an alphabetical frame of mind, Noah and I made off to
www.kidsclick.org. KidsClick! is a database of over 6400 sites gathered together
by librarians, which means that it doesn't cover the entire Web. Although it offers
a search tool—discussed later in this section—it also offers a handy alphabetical
way to find our man Mr. Burbank.

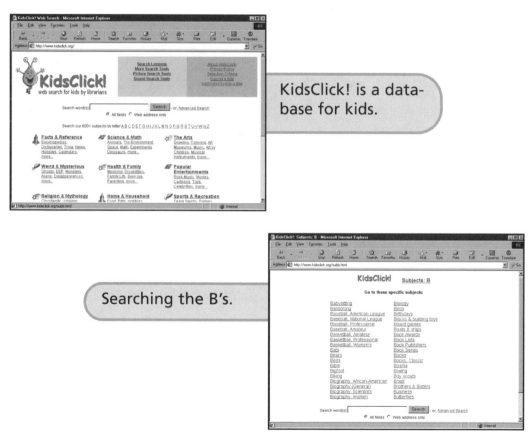

KidsClick! is a data-base for kids.

Searching the B's.

Although the letter "B" didn't deposit us at Luther Burbank's garden gate, we
were able to narrow down our search to "Biographies, scientists" and get some
good leads to his life story.

Sorted Subject Directories

Once you move from the alphabet, kids sites are organized in a variety of ways and offer a number of tools to locate the goods on your topic. Many are organized by subject matter, where people literally go through the World Wide Web sorting out topics that they think will be useful (and appropriate) for kids' use. Some of the best that let you sort from general to specific topics to find what you're after are:

KidsClick! (sites selected by librarians) ....**www.kidsclick.org**
Yahooligans (for kids 7-12) ....**www.yahooligans.com**
Awesome Library (16,000 sites for kids) .... **www.awesomelibrary.org**
ThinkQuest Library (educational sites by students).........................**www.thinkquest.com**
Berit's Best Sites (1,000 sites for kids under 12) ....**www.beritsbest.com**

Noah and I decide to take our search to Yahooligans!, a Kids' directory site sponsored by Yahoo!, a leading directory. I opt to go for the Science and Nature category, but Noah—always thinking—says that we're looking for information about who Luther is, not science. And, as usual, he turns out to be right. Our eventual pathway through the site locates Luther according to this road map.

Around the World>Countries>United States>History>Biographies.
And then, at long last, Luther.

Want More?

Several Web sites evaluate search sites, offer hot searching tips, and offer comprehensive lists of specialized Web sites. Check out:

Easy Searcher ....**www.easysearcher.com**
Search Engines ....**www.searchengines.com**
Search engine watch ....**www.searchenginewatch.com**

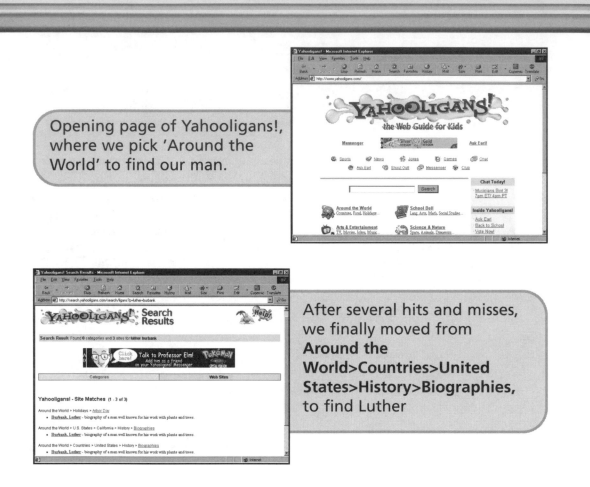

Opening page of Yahooligans!, where we pick 'Around the World' to find our man.

After several hits and misses, we finally moved from **Around the World>Countries>United States>History>Biographies,** to find Luther

It's probably clear that this wasn't an easy search: five clicks and quite a few discussions on whether we were actually ever going to dig our man up (no garden pun intended). We would have been smart to do a keyword search right off, since we knew what we wanted (see Keywords below).

This is a useful lesson. Directories are good when you want to find something, but you don't know its exact name. For example, what if Noah's assignment was to find a scientist who was involved with plants? A directory might help find some important botanists, one of whom might be Luther Burbank.

Keyword Searches

One thing about a subject search directory like Yahooligans!: it takes a lot of clicking to get your answer. You probably noticed the number of sites Noah and I had to pass through before we actually reached Mr. Burbank.

A faster method is to use keyword or phrase searching. You simply put in what you're searching for and the site goes in search of :

→ Subjects with the word or words entered,

→ Web site names that contain the word or words,

→ Web site descriptions that contain that word or words, or

→ Actual Web pages that have that word or words someplace on the page.

Keyword Math & Boolean Logic

To use search engines effectively, it helps to apply techniques that narrow results and push the most relevant pages to the top of the results list.

When you put in more than one word into a search space, the software is faced with a decision. Should it find sites where all the words appear? Or should it find sites even if only one of the words appears? One way to narrow your search is to use a little Boolean logic and keyword math.

To start, break down your topic into key concepts. For example, if we want to find out about Luther Burbank's research with plumcots the keywords might be:

Luther Burbank plumcots

Most search software is designed to work as if there was an invisible "AND" between keywords. This tells the search engine to retrieve Web pages containing all the keywords. For example, when you put in "Luther Burbank plumcots" the engine interprets this as:

Luther AND Burbank AND plumcots MUST APPEAR.

Linking search terms with "OR" tells the search engine to retrieve Web pages containing ANY and ALL keywords:

Luther OR Burbank OR plumcots MUST APPEAR.

This search will give you more results, since it will give you all pages where Luther, Burbank, or plumcots appear, individually or in combination. "OR" expands you results.

Linking words with "AND NOT" tells the search engine to retrieve Web pages that contain one keyword but not the other. It's particularly useful when searching for a single term often found with another—such as Sonny AND NOT Cher or Salt AND NOT Pepper. But say you were running a search to find out about the California city of Burbank and didn't want any pesky Luther's showing up. With the addition of "AND NOT" the search engine sees:

Burbank AND NOT Luther MUST APPEAR.

Here's the cool part: for many engines, you don't need to write words. This is where the math comes in. The phrase "+Luther+Burbank+plumcots" works like the "AND." And when it comes to "AND NOT," a minus sign will do: "Burbank-Luther" will keep our man at bay.

Now that you know search engines can add and subtract, guess what—they can also multiply. For example, if you want to find everything about Luther Burbank's research in plumcots, you could (as we've said), write "Luther+Burbank+plumcots." That will return all the pages that include those words on them, but they may be scattered throughout the page instead of linked together in a phrase.

A phrase—or multiplied—search avoids this problem. By putting quotation marks around a phrase such as "Luther Burbank plumcots," the search engine will return only pages that have all the words in the exact order shown, guaranteeing a result that will be much more on target.

Once you get the basics of search engine math, you can jump to more advanced navigations. Say you want only information about Luther Burbank the man, without anything on his plant research (Luther, by the way, was quite a philosopher outside of his botanical studies). To find those aspects, you might try "Luther+Burbank-plants" or a little multiplication and subtraction: "Luther Burbank-plants."

Although search sites may appear to operate similarly, the truth is that each has individual quirks. For example, Alta Vista has an automatic phrase detector, which means you don't need to use quotation marks. You will need to use the + symbol with quotation marks at Google.

To learn how your selected search engine operates, take time to read the search assistance features offered on each site.

Boolean Logic

"Boolean" refers to a system of logical thought developed by the English mathematician and computer pioneer, George Boole (1815-64). Boole's book, *The Mathematical Analysis of Logic*, published in 1840, showed that logic could be exhibited as an algebraic equation. Today, Boole's several texts on symbolic logic are used not only in math, but in teaching information theory, graph theory, computer science, and artificial intelligence research. In Boolean searching, an "and" between two words (such as a "pear AND apple") indicates a search for documents containing both words, while an "or" ("a pear OR apple") indicates you're looking for documents containing either word. (For more on George Boole, see Jones Telecommunications and Multimedia Encyclopedia at **www.digitalcentury.com/encyclo/update/boole.html**.)

Gentlemen, start your engines...

What greets you when you open your computer? If you first hit the site of your Web provider (like MSN), realize that life online doesn't have to start there. You can reset your opening page. For parents interested in what their kids do online, setting it to a kid-friendly search engine or educational Web portal can put kids on the right path the moment they log on.

Visual Search

Weary with words, Noah and I decide to head for something completely different: search directories at MamaMedia (**www.MaMaMedia.com**). The engines are part of a larger educational site packed with games, projects, and communication tools for kids to share and publish their work. The site is based on what its founder, Idit Harel, calls the 3X's—express, explore, and exchange. Bringing these educational ideas to search engines, we leave Luther behind for a moment to do just those things.

Entering the site, we log in and enter the Romp area where we're offered two engines: Sandwich Shop and Web Party. We head for the bread, where we're offered 'world on rye,' 'kids' deluxe,' 'healthfood hero,' 'nature burger,' 'showtime combo,' and 'make your own.'

"This is a search engine?"

I urge Noah to give it a chance. Watching our calories, he heads for the healthfood hero. Once we click, the screen divides into four strips, the top of which offer five new choices. We pick outdoor places, which in turn brings up four new picks. Each time, we notice that the number of possible selections narrows until we land on a Web site.

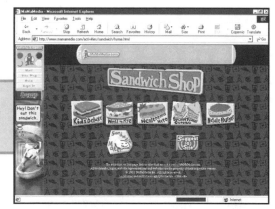

Now for something different, a transparent search site from MaMaMedia.

Sampling Search Sites

Counting conservatively, there are over 600 search sites on the Internet. The larger engines—like Google, Alta Vista, and Yahoo!—offer the most indexed pages, but if you have a specialized topic, it might be worth trying out smaller sites.

Although this doesn't look like any other directory we've tried before, Noah and I realize that as we click, we're building a visual model of a directory. With each click, we're narrowing down our choices, until finally we settle on a single site—one of the carefully kid-friendly destinations selected by MaMaMedia.com.

While MaMaMedia.com's tool isn't really an effective search engine for anything but the most random research, it's a fun and graphic demonstration of how directory sites work. And the area can lead kids to sites that cover blue cheese, blues music, blueberries or bluefish. If you're a search 'Newbie' this can be a great way to get a quick, visually appealing demonstration of how search engines and directories operate.

Luther Burbank: Found

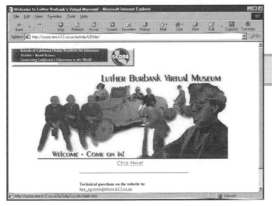

Mr. Burbank, we presume…

Refreshed by our visit to MaMaMedia, we really start to dig. And we hit pay dirt: The Luther Burbank Virtual Museum (**http://score.rims.k12.ca.us/ activity/LBSite/**). Along with a tour of the Luther Burbank gardens and museum, it offers a number of hands-on experiments to help you follow in Luther's footsteps.

What we discovered was that using grafting techniques, Luther Burbank created and introduced over 200 different varieties of fruits and nuts. He is perhaps best known for creating nectarines, plumcots (a cross between apricots and plums), freestone peaches, and over 100 different types of plums and prunes. His most famous plum is probably the Santa Rosa Plum.

But alas, no watermelon.

Seedless Watermelons: Uncovered

Fifty years ago, a Japanese scientist developed the first seedless watermelon. His work has been carried on for the past 14 years by Don Maynard, a researcher at the University of Florida. Luther Burbank had nothing much to do with it, but Noah turns out to have had it right from the start. Seedless varieties of fruit, including watermelon, are sweeter, which doesn't explain why the watermelon that started this whole thing wasn't. (For more information on Maynard and the seedless watermelon, see **www.napa.ufl.edu/digest/old/1998-99/watermelon.htm**.) Next search: the Square watermelon...

"I'm hungry," Noah sighed.

Notes of a searcher

It's one thing to locate material online; it's another to know if it's worthwhile, critically sound, and valid. Part of the wonder of the Web is its plentitude and disorganization. While search engines can guide you, working with smaller kids' engines that are vetted by librarians or experts like Mama Media educators has the advantage of raising fewer questions about the accuracy of what you're looking at. To help your child, ask questions when you reach a site: how old is the material? Who wrote it? When was the site last updated? You might also want to check information against that found in a local or school library to see how it measures up.

Remember: just because it's on the Web doesn't make it true.

Directories vs. Search Engines

Compiled by human beings, **directories** are organized by topic, moving from general to specific areas. While some have familiar plug-in "search" functions that let you enter a keyword, they aren't true search engines. But directories work great if:

→ You're new to the Net.

→ You're looking for a list of subjects assembled by experts. For kids' lists, this often means librarians, who handpick areas under each topic.

→ When you only have a general idea of what you're looking for.

Search Engines are compiled by computer programs called "spiders" or "bots" that scan and index Web sites by title pages, Web addresses, and text. Tap into a search engine when:

→ You know precisely what you're looking for.

→ You want to combine terms. (You can combine keywords to narrow the search using special search techniques.)

Project Search

→ The MadSci Network at **www.madsci.org.** To call this site cool isn't enough: it's frigid. Along with edible labs, a virtual human, and over 800 scientific experts available to answer your pressing questions, these pages feature a "Random Knowledge Generator" which archives answers to questions they've answered. It's like a search engine gone bonkers—answering everything from how to save a mallard duck egg found in a swimming pool to whether one poisonous snake can poison another. Enjoy!

→ Powers of Ten **http://micro.magnet.fsu.edu/primer/java/scienceopticsu/powersof10** Click your way from the Milky Way to a proton, all from the comfort of your keyboard. A search for things of different sizes that even the smallest Webmaster can conduct.

→ Travlang's Foreign Languages for Travelers **(www.travlang.com/languages).** Eighty different tongues to twist complete with pronunciations. Enter your native language, then count your way through Armenian, shop in Dagaare, and tell time in Yiddish.

Hyperlink or links

A hyperlink or link is a fast way of getting around the Web. When you click on underlined or highlighted words or pictures, you'll automatically be taken to the "linked" site. This means that you won't have to enter a new Web address (URL) every time you want to go from here to there.

Searching for Search History?

What do Archie, Veronica, and Jughead have to do with search engines? Find out at

A History of Search Engines:
www.wiley.com/legacy/compbooks/sonnenreich/history.html

Top Search Engines and their Histories can be found at:
www.dcn.davis.ca.us/~vctinney/searchen.htm

Projects: Kids Search Sites to Explore

→ Ask Jeeves for Kids at **www.ajkids.com** is a natural language site. This means that rather than search through topics or use keywords, you simply put in your question, "Who is Luther Burbank?" and click search. The program takes you to your questions.

→ Go to ArtKidsRule at **www.artkidsrule.com** to explore a multimedia directory, along with artist tutorials, art quizzes for kids, and previews of the Sunday comics.

→ The Amazing Picture Machine has images of everything from tornadoes to Texas. Check out this photo archive at **www.ncrtec.org/picture.htm**.

→ Run by Marshal Brain (yes, that's his real name), How Stuff Works takes on the animal, vegetable and mineral worlds and explains it all. Recent topics cover how barrier islands work, how lethal injections work, and how the brain works. Recommended for teens (some topics unsuitable for small fry). See **www.howstuffworks.com**.

→ An encyclopedia of mythology, legends and folklore can be found at **www.pantheon.org/mythica.html**.

→ Biographies of inventors and inventions from the Smithsonian Museum in Washington D.C. can be found at **www.si.edu/resource/faq/nmah/invent.htm**.

→ Fact Monster—an online dictionary, encyclopedia, and all purpose homework helper is located at **www.factmonster.com**.

→ All Elvis, all the time. Need we say more? **www.ElvisSearch.com**.

→ Dictionaries online include Merriam-Webster Online (**www.m-w.com**) and Wordsmyth (**www.wordsmyth.net**).

→ Find the perfect—or imperfect—quote of your dreams at **www.quoteland.com**. Or draw from Amazon.com's large selection of quotations that range from the silly to the profound at **www.QuoteWorld.org**.

Email

Chapter 3

E-mail

Cheap, easy-to-use, and much faster than "snail mail"—regular Post Office delivery to Internet users—e-mail is electronic messages sent from one computer to another. As one of the first practical ways to use the Internet, e-mail began and remains one of its most widely popular features.

How does e-mail work? In a way, it's not that different from regular mail. As letters make their way across country, they stop at different post offices and get sorted until they finally reach the right mailbox. E-mail passes from one computer—known as a mail server—to another as it travels over the Internet. Eventually, it arrives at the destination mail server, where it is stored in an electronic mailbox until you retrieve it. You can also attach pictures, files, and software packages to e-mail messages.

To get e-mail, you must have a connection to the Internet and access to a mail server that can forward your mail. Both Netscape and Microsoft include an e-mail utility with their Web browsers.

E-mail Accounts

You can get free e-mail accounts from the sites listed below. If you already have an account, you may still want to apply for a second e-mail to use for e-commerce or for your kids. (Some of these services also offer free junk busting software to prevent the dreaded spam.)

E-mail.com ....**www.email.com**
Hotmail ....**www.hotmail.com**
ProntoMail ....**www.prontomail.com**
Yahoo!Mail..**http://mail.yahoo.com**

Sending and Receiving E-mail

Like regular mail, e-mail operates by sending and receiving messages in care of addresses. Let's examine a specific e-mail address. Take, for example: **tonypizzaman@restaurant.com.** How to translate this? Simple. E-mail sent to this address will go to the user, tonypizzaman, at (@) his electronic mailbox (restaurant), which is a commercial (.com) domain.

When you're ready to send Tony a note, the process remains pretty uncomplicated. If you're using MSN Outlook, you can bring up a blank mail form from the tool bar, then enter the address beside "To" and a brief description of your message in the space marked "Subject". Then click down to the body of the e-mail and compose your message.

The address (tonypizza-man@restaurant.com) and the subject (Re: Anchovy and Pineapple Pizza) appears in the upper or header portion, while the message is located in the lower or body of the e-mail.

How E-mail Is Organized

Netscape Messengers and Outlook Express organize e-mail into folders. These include:

Inbox...Messages you have received.
Outbox/Unsent Messages.....................Messages composed that are ready to send.
Sent...Copies of messages you've mailed.
Deleted/Trash...Messages deleted from any other folder.

Click on "Actions", and pick "new mail." Then type the recipient's address and a brief title that describes your message. Then move down to the subject space, and insert your message.

Once you've composed your immortal words to Tony, click "Send" to transfer the e-mail to the outbox. There, depending on your system, it will either be sent immediately or wait a bit before taking off.

Messages lined in the "Outbox" waiting to be sent.

When you want to reply to your own incoming e-mail, simply click on the bold face message, hit the "Reply" button, and compose your message. When you hit "Send" the mail server will automatically whisk the message back to the original sender.

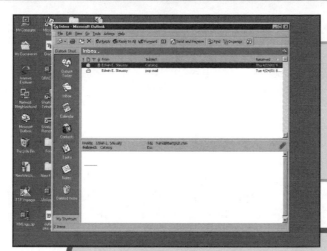

Microsoft Outlook Express Inbox shows messages waiting to be read in bold type. Click onto any message to open your mail.

Return to Sender

Messages sent as e-mail go to your mail server, which then determines the best route to get it to the recipient. Sometimes, however, the message is undeliverable. In that case, the mail will be 'bounced' back to you by the mail administrator, which will also include a reason why the mail couldn't get through. Common reasons include:

→ **Incorrect address:** Error messages reading "User unknown" or "Host unknown" alerts you to an incorrect address error. Check your typing: even a single mistake can prevent delivery.

→ **Software errors:** Look for the message "Connection timed out."

→ **Hardware problems.** These are messages such as "Connection refused" or "Network unreachable."

Finding E-mail Addresses

To protect their customers' privacy, most Internet Service Providers don't register e-mail addresses. If you want to be included in an e-mail online directory, you'll have to do it yourself. Forms are available at a number of sites that offer e-mail address searches.

If you can't find an e-mail address on a Web site, you can try My E-Mail Address (**http://my.email.address.is**). This provides a sort of meta-search through several other online directories, including Yahoo! People! (**http://people.yahoo.com**), Switchboard (**www.switchboard.com**), WhoWhere (**www.whowhere.lycos.com**), Infospace (**http://infospace.com**), and Internet Address Finder (**www.iaf.net**). Remember that different sites have different e-mail databases, so if you come up dry on one, try another.

Mind Your Manners

Netiquette is the name for minding your p's and q's when communicating via e-mail, on bulletin boards or in chat rooms. The basic rules here aren't that different from other forms of communication, but you may want to make sure your kids know how to behave. Without facial expressions or body language, others can easily misinterpret text-only communication online.

➔ Be concise and come to the point. When it comes to sending e-mail messages, the shorter the better. Think of it as a long-distance telephone conversation.

➔ Avoid too much punctuation. This goes triple for exclamation points. One will get your excitement across.

➔ Keep capital letters where they belong. Online, TYPING EVERYTHING IN CAPITALS is the equivalent of shouting in another person's ear.

➔ Don't flame others. "Flaming" is a written insult, which can quickly fan into a "flame war," or exchange of insults.

➔ Don't send anything private in an e-mail. One person can easily forward your message to another and pretty soon your love letter is all over the Net.

➔ Don't send another person's message on without permission. Even if it's just information, it's best to ask first.

➔ Before you hit the 'send' button, check your message for spelling, grammar, etc.

➔ Try to include a subject title in your message so the recipient knows who it's from, and what the message is about.

➔ Don't spam (send lots of irrelevant or moderately relevant e-mail to one or many recipients). E-mail is so effortless; it's easy to get carried away. Check up on your child's e-mail production; it's not nice to spam grandma.

Safety & Privacy Tips

E-mail, bulletin boards, and other forms of 'chat' can help you and your kids keep in touch not only with friends and families, but with teachers, mentors, and pen pals. But before you let your children go online to e-mail, follow the rules of the Internet road:

→ Talk to your child about who they meet online.

→ For younger children, you may want to share your child's e-mail account and password. Or, set up a separate joint account for you and your child.

→ Remind your child never to agree to meet anyone online without your specific permission.

→ Complain to senders about unsolicited e-mail and to your Internet Service Provider about any unwanted e-mail or spam.

→ Remind your child that once e-mail is sent, anyone can read it.

→ Once you send e-mail, it's the property of the person who receives it. This means they can pass your message along to anyone they please. The moral? Don't send messages that you would be embarrassed for anyone else to read.

Abbreviations

One fun feature of communication online is the number of abbreviations that have arisen to deal with the concise nature of the form. Some are familiar to office workers (FYI or for your information), while others can get a bit exotic (ROTFL or rolling on the floor laughing). The best bet is to limit your use of them; otherwise you can risk being misunderstood. But they can spice up e-mail, IM, or chat.

AFK	away from keyboard	**IMHO**	in my humble opinion
BCNU	be seeing you	**JK**	just kidding
BTW	by the way	**LOL**	laughing out loud
BFN	bye for now	**OBO**	or best offer
BRB	be right back	**ROTFL**	rolling on the floor laughing
FWIW	for what it's worth	**RTFM**	read the freaking manual
G	grin	**TIA**	thanks in advance
IIRC	if I remember correctly	**TTFN**	ta ta for now
IMO	in my opinion	**TTYL**	talk to you later

Viruses

It came by e-mail, an innocent little message wishing me a Happy New Year. And when I opened the attachment, I was greeted by the most adorable animated fireworks. But within an hour, my computer files had developed a number of odd tics, my e-mail was incapacitated, and I realized I had fallen victim to that great fear of computer users—my very own virus.

By now, most computer users have heard of, or had a brush with, a virus: a piece of self-replicating computer software that can wreak havoc with your computer. Many of these viruses—such as the famous 1999 Melissa virus that led to the closing down of Microsoft's e-mail networks or the "I love you" bug—enter via an e-mail attachment, while others come directly onto your PC. In most cases, the sender doesn't realize that the attachment is infected.

Viruses can be very destructive. When, for example, a recipient of the Melissa virus opened an e-mail attachment, the virus quickly hijacked the local Microsoft Outlook e-mail system and mailed itself to the first fifty entries of the unsuspecting recipient's address book. What started as a small ripple of extra mail eventually became a flood, overwhelming the capacity of the mail servers to handle the overload and eventually causing the entire system to fail.

How to protect yourself? Anti-virus software will scan your system each time you log on and check for viruses. However, since new viruses are always on the prowl, you'll need to update the anti-virus software so it will be able to detect new ones. You can also teach your kids, and remind yourself, never to open e-mail attachments that arrive from unfamiliar sources and to ask your permission before downloading new pieces of software. This bit of advice is so important that I'll repeat myself: Never open e-mail attachments from unfamiliar sources, and make sure that software you or your children download is from a trusted source.

The Challenge:
A Brush with Power E-mail

Given the profusion of folks online, the audience for e-mail is limitless: grandmothers, grandfathers, aunts, uncles, best friends, teachers, and on and on. But Noah and I decided to aim a little higher up the food chain for our first joint e-mail: a quick note to the Commander in Chief, our Prez. Our request was simple: we wanted permission to play baseball on the White House lawn.

We had seen a report on CNN about Little Leaguers holding batting practice behind the Rose Garden and figured we might get in on the action. Our team, after all, had been smokin' up the local diamonds all spring, and we were ready for the Show. Confident that our President, a former major league owner, couldn't refuse our earnest request (we'd even bring our own bats and balls), we took up our keyboard to compose a message.

Using his new searching skills, Noah found the e-mail address to 1600 Pennsylvania Avenue without any trouble. A quick trip to the White House Web site yielded the e-mail addresses for both the President and Vice-President.

Noah opened our e-mail program, pulled up a new message form, and began typing. With care he tapped in the official address, our subject, and his request, then—after a quick proofreading by Mom—hit 'Send'.

Aware that the White House might have a few other things on its collective mind, we were prepared to wait. But, to our surprise, e-mail proved right up there with the speed of light. Within seconds, the e-mail signal chimed, and we faced the Big Reply.

"He must really like us!" Noah crowed.

Well, not quite. While we didn't have to cool our heels, what we learned was that while getting to the White House by e-mail is simple, getting around the White House answering service isn't. Rather than our anticipated offer for Noah, me, and our fellow Little League teammates, parents, coaches and assorted hangers-on to board Air Force One for the on-site baseball field, we found ourselves parsing a disheartening form letter informing us that while the President appreciates mail, he receives too much mail to read, let alone answer, every piece.

Not a word about our baseball team. Or our trip on Air Force One.

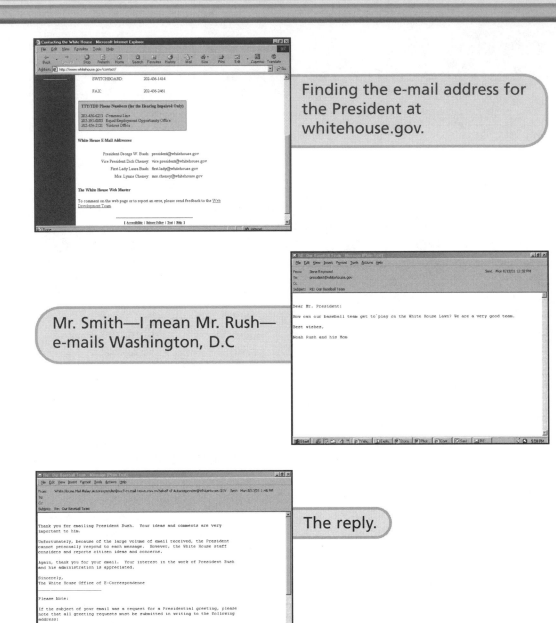

Finding the e-mail address for the President at whitehouse.gov.

Mr. Smith—I mean Mr. Rush— e-mails Washington, D.C

The reply.

Talking to the Big Guys

Although we had bombed with our President, we wondered if it's as easy to commune with other world leaders via e-mail. It turned out it is. At **www.trytel.com/~aberdeen** we found listings for "Monarchs, Presidents, Prime Ministers, and Provincial Governors from Afghanistan to Zimbabwe." Lots of Web sites and ways to connect to leaders here, but the sheer numbers were a little overwhelming (and did they play baseball in Zimbabwe?).

Noah was all for abandoning ship for a game of running bases, when we stumbled upon a great site that leads us straight to the top, KidsCom (**www.kidscom.com**).

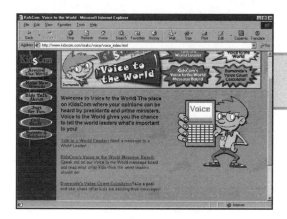

Kids.com gives kids a chance to speak to world leaders.

Along with a chance to find regular-kid pen pals from around the globe, this site offers a unique chance for children to e-mail leaders around the world with their opinions about important issues from space exploration to the environment here on Planet Earth. Unfortunately, inviting our Little League team did not come up among the choices of prepackaged messages, but we're certain that's an oversight soon to be remedied.

Global Pen Pals

So, who needs famous politicians, anyway? What about plain old super kids? In addition to offering the chance to commune with opinion makers, there are a number of sites that give kids a chance to pick up a global pen pal. Many link 'keypals' by hobbies, interests, and age.

One electronic pen pal site is Kids' Space Connection (**www.ks-connection.org**). Along with matching up kids by interests and age, the site offers a cool country search engine that lets you find a pen pal by location. Worth looking at is also the Cyberkids site for pen pals, **www.cyberkids.com**, where pen pals are divided by age and sex. Teens might want to check out the cyber café, where older kids chat.

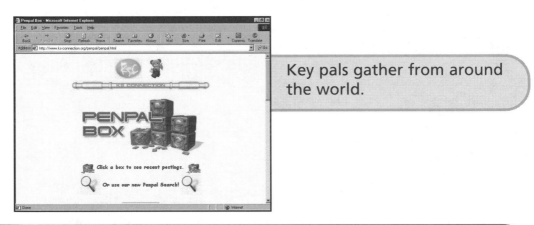

Key pals gather from around the world.

E-mail Extras

Sometimes, plain old e-mail simply won't do. To buff up your message power, try some of these special mail services offered free on the Web.

http://postcards.www.media.mit.edu/Postcards/cardrack.html
Vermeer, Allen Ginsberg, or carp (yes, the fish) await you in this eclectic selection of fabulous postcards waiting to be sent to your nearest and dearest. (We particularly liked the life cycle of the termite.)

www.bluemountain.com
Free cards are offered for every occasion from birthdays to National Pickle Week.

www.e-cards.com
An electronic postcard site with a twist: for every card you mail, a donation is made towards nature preservation. Mail well and do well at the same time.

Meeting the Masses: Lists

One of the most interesting uses of e-mail is connecting you with lists of people who share common interests. You can add your address to some lists by sending a request to the mailing list administrator. A list that is administered in this way is called a "list server." Going onto a listserv means messages from other subscribers will be automatically sent to your electronic mailbox. Some offer digests culled from a day's or week's discussion as well.

Listservs are great for chatting and meeting new people who share your passions—whether it is for Little League baseball or Harry Potter books. One of the most comprehensive lists of listserv groups and newsletters (which can be sent to subscribers via listserv software) can be found at **www.topica.com**, where you can join groups devoted to Ninja Turtles, kids' videos, or raising show dogs, among other topics. Another good source is Vivian Neou's List of Lists at **http://catalog.com/vivian/interest-group-search.html**.

Fresh from our baseball adventure with the Prez, Noah and I decided to take a chance on joining a baseball forum at Topica. To join, we simply sent the list administrator an e-mail with the message "subscribe Noah Rush" in the body. In most cases, this will get your name added to the list, and within a few minutes, you'll receive a confirmation. To let the administrator know that you still intend to join, you'll be asked to verify the confirmation, either by sending a fast "OK" back or by clicking to a Web site that confirms your membership. The message will also explain how to add your voice to the discussion, how to un-subscribe, and other details about the list.

As in regular e-mail, kids need to be careful when using listservs. It's best to use a parent's address, and not to give out any personal information online. To protect kids, there are several "kids only" mail groups. Two—one for kids under thirteen and one for kids over 13 but below age 18—are offered on America Online. (Send an e-mail to **KIDS-request@LISTSERV.AOL.COM** to subscribe.) Parents are permitted to register kids under 13, but adults are not welcome to participate on the list.

One of the best places for kids to join in listserv mania is Kidlink (**www.kidlink.org**). A worldwide network connecting kids, Kidlink offers a chat café, pen pals, and listserv conferences that can be built around educational projects. Many classroom teachers have used Kidlink in school projects.

One project, called "Who Am I?" gives kids around the world a chance to introduce themselves, and to discuss their cultures. Another titled "I Have A Dream" encourages kids to come up with a dream idea to improve the future of the world, then to figure out practical methods to make their vision a reality. The Kidlink listserv is limited to children and teens, but the group also provides listserv "conferences" for interested teachers and parents to keep track of their kids' interests and progress on the projects. Detailed information on joining the Kidlink listservs appears at **www.kidlink.org/english/general/sub.html**.

Once you've added your name to a listserv, all you have to do is jump in, and then wait for responses to arrive.

This brings up one problem of joining a listserv that all prospective users need to be hyperaware of: message overload. Depending on the passions involved and the topic at hand, listservs can become quite chatty. At times we're talking fairly massive quantities of e-mail.

Noah and I—mainly I since we used my e-mail address (a good safety tip for kids who are starting out on listservs to preserve privacy)—learned this the hard way. Innocently logging online one morning after the All-Star team was selected in July, I blinked to find 11 new messages from hitherto unknown baseball listserv buddies. What had inflamed the group? Joe Torre, manager of the 2000 World Champion New York Yankees, apparently had seen fit to name seven of his players to the 2001 All-Star team. What followed was listserv pandemonium with folks from Chicago, Tokyo and elsewhere trying to second-guess, defend, out-smart and simply refuse to believe Mr. Torre's decision. Ninety-two messages later I finally gave up and signed off.

One tip: if you're away from your computer for a few days, you might want to briefly leave the list, which usually involves sending a simple "unsubscribe Noah Rush (put in your name)" to the list administrator (or the address given to you by the administrator to cancel your subscription). This prevents any chance of returning home to find 300 or more oh-so-urgent messages from your fellow baseball (or Ninja Turtle) fans. You should also consider learning a little more about your e-mail software, most of which allow you to filter incoming mail into separate folders or mailboxes.

Despite my crowded mailbox, I really encourage you and your kids to give a listserv a try. For one, it's great to get e-mail. And, unlike the White House (hint, hint), listserv folks actually want to hear your questions and want to answer them. Having joined several listservs, I've found that participants tend to stay on topic, and—perhaps best of all—it's nice knowing that other people can get as obsessed about those darned Yankees as we two Mets fans. Speaking as a Mom, it's a good lesson for Noah, and a chance to develop his summer passion for baseball with fellow fans around the world. Who needs the Rose Garden—let's play ball!

Projects:
E-Mailing on a Lazy (or Busy) Afternoon

Ask Dr. Universe
(www.wsu.edu/DrUniverse/Contents.html)

Have a question you can't find the answer to? Questioned all the usual suspects, looked in all the old familiar places, and come up dry? Dr. Universe is a cool cat with access to all of the expertise of Washington State University. She answers questions about science, sure, but also about anything else via an e-mail form on her site.

Snail Mail vs. E-Mail

Know anyone in a far away state or—even better—a foreign country? Get them to mail you a letter by standard post (snail mail) or airmail, and then try to predict when it might arrive. To fatten the fun (or the penny pool), try to get other friends or family members to give their best guesses. When the letter—finally—arrives, predict how long an e-mail might take, set your bets, and then compare your ideas to the results.

Meet My Monster

A popular and fun e-mail exercise used by many classrooms is to describe a monster, then send your description to a friend, who then, following your depiction, draws a picture of your creation. When it's done, they can either post their drawing on a Web site or snail mail it back so you can see how close they came to realizing your written description. Fine tuning the monster messages helps sharpen descriptive skills on both sides of the post.

Our Favorite Emoticons

Emoticons or "smilies" replace visual and auditory cues in regular one-on-one conversation. Perhaps the most common is the ubiquitous "smilie" or : -). Turn your head to the left and you should spot the happy face. Typically these are found at the end of sentences and usually refer to the sentence before.

;-)	**Wink (light sarcasm)**	:-P	**Wry smile**
:- |	**Indifference**	;-}	**Leer**
:->	**Devilish grin (heavy sarcasm)**	:-Q	**Smoker**
o:-)	**Innocent remark**	:-e	**Disappointment**
>:-)	**Devilish remark**	:-@	**Scream**
:~)	**User has a cold**	:-O	**Yell or open-mouthed**
8-)	**Eye-glasses or wide-eyed**	:-X	**Close-mouthed**
:-D	**Shock or surprise**	:-*	**Drunk**
:-/	**Perplexed**	:-{}	**Wears lipstick**
:-(	**Frown or anger**	:-]	**Smirk**

Did You Know?

Unsolicited e-mail is called spam, and if you put your e-mail on a registration form for any services online, you can (and probably will) be "spammed." Spam is the trademarked name of a Hormel meat product used to feed soldiers during World War II, though e-mail spam takes its name from a skit on the '70s British television comedy, "Monty Python's Flying Circus. ("Well, we have Spam, Tomato & Spam, Egg & Spam, Egg, Bacon & Spam...")

To avoid spam:

→ **Don't give your primary e-mail address to any commercial service.** Instead, sign up for a free e-mail service like Hotmail (**www.hotmail.com**) or Juno (**www.juno.com**) and use that address for online purchases. You can also use a different account for each purchase: mygap@hotmail.com.

→ **Don't agree to receive free information from a commercial site:** it's an invitation to spam.

→ **Never reply to a junk e-mail message;** offers to "unsubscribe" may be hidden requests to verify your address.

Chat Rooms
and
Discussion
Boards
Chapter 4

Chat Rooms and Discussion Boards

Back in the old days (say ten years ago), most people viewed computers as super at number crunching, but not much to brag about in the social communications department. As any teen with an Internet connection and access to Instant Messaging (IM) will tell you, times have changed. Today, computers are prime communicators. Day and night, fingers fly on keyboards around the world. Surfers post the latest and greatest waves, teachers' trade secret tips on keeping classrooms lively, while kids compare music downloads and Game Boy prowess.

Or, as my 16-year-old son might put it, "Chat is the Man."

For adults, chat rooms offer an infinite variety of connections and fill diverse roles. Chat rooms can act as support groups, offer up to the minute news stories, or serve as research (or romantic) tools. But for kids and teens, chat has an additional—and sometimes to adults, puzzling—function.

"I like to think as kids' chat as the equivalent of 'hanging out online'," says Steven Jones, Ph.D., professor of Communications at the University of Illinois at Chicago. "Not a lot of what adults might see as having 'value' goes on in kids' chat rooms, but to kids who use it, it obviously serves a necessary purpose."

Keep in Mind

→ Never share personal information such as your real name, city, phone number, age, or e-mail address.

Netiquette

→ **No caps.** Speaking in all caps IS LIKE SHOUTING.
→ **Be concise.** This is particularly important on IRC chat, where flooding—sending too much information to the channel at once—is considered bad form. Hold your entries to three lines or less.
→ **Limit greetings.** When you enter a chat room, you don't need to greet everyone. One "Hello!" is enough. Also, don't expect anybody to greet you back. On a channel with 20 people that would mean a screen filled with hellos. If you must say hello to somebody you know, do it with a private message. The same applies to good-byes.
→ **Respect others.** Many sites reserve the right to remove those who advocate or encourage expressions of violent, hateful, bigoted, racist, or profane actions.
→ **Play nice.** Persistent harassing remarks or off-topic comments or flooding the chat room or boards with inappropriate remarks can lead to expulsion from some boards.

Internet Relay Chat or "Chat Rooms"

> **{Sam}** Hey, are you new to IRC too?
> **{Jake}** I dont agree there :-(
> **{East-r}** Can she give me that too?? I couldnt find it before
> *** East-r smiles**
> **{Sam }** Nope, I just have a simple question... I think...

Entering an Internet Relay Chat (IRC) room for the first time is a lot like getting lost in a foreign city where no one speaks your language. It's disorienting, confusing, and probably will leave you longing for the safe confines and understandable parameters of home. Yet if you hang around long enough to pick up a little of the lingo, and meet a group of sympathetic 'newbies' like yourself, it can eventually be a great way to meet new people from around the world. Don't be afraid to talk, but it pays to "lurk"—hang around as a guest to listen and observe—before you jump in.

IRC chat takes place in specific "chat rooms" or "Channels" in real time. Chats can be ongoing conversations, or scheduled for a particular time or duration. Some chats are focused around a topic or a guest speaker. Some chat rooms are just open conversations, where everyone has a pretty much equal role. Other rooms are moderated where there is a "speaker" who is leading the discussion. Some rooms have chaperons or monitors who are responsible for maintaining order. The monitor can kick someone who is acting in an inappropriate manner out of the room, but he or she may be able to act only after the fact. The monitor can't, however, prevent you (or your child) from going off to a private chat area with a person who might do you harm. Neither can the monitor stop you or your child from typing information that could put you in danger.

While e-mail can remind you of Post Office 'snail mail,' online chat can perhaps best be compared to speaking on the phone. But rather than actually speaking, you 'chat' with others via typed messages that are sent back and forth over the computer network. Messages fly quickly between everyone in the chat room as they respond to one another. But unlike a telephone, everyone in the chat room can see everything everybody else types.

Getting Connected

There are two basic ways to connect to chat online: using a Java "applet" or downloading software to enter a chat channel.

Applets

Many teen and kid Web sites offer an IRC client Java "applet"—a little program application that can connect you with a chat without bothering your service provider. Noah and I found one good and fast connection on KidsCom at **www.KidsCom.com.**

IRC Software

If you want to enter a chat room that doesn't support an applet connection, you need to connect to IRC on your own. To do this, you'll need an Internet connection, and a program that permits you to join up with others to talk. While many different programs exist, the most widely used are either mIRC (m stands for the name of the fellow that wrote the program, Khaled Mardam-Bey, and you'll recognize the IRC) or PIRCH.

Either of these two programs can be downloaded at **www.irchelp.org**.

The first time you run mIRC or PIRCH you have to fill in some information about yourself (your name, e-mail address, nickname, IP address, and Local Host name) under File/Setup/IRC Servers and Local Info, as well as the IRC server with which you want to connect. It's usually best to connect to a geographically close server.

Fill in the blanks for mIRC.

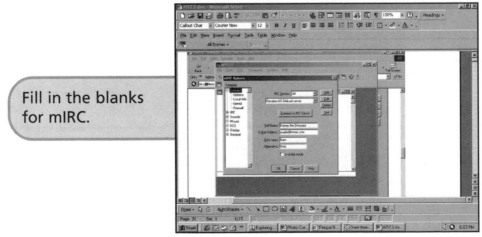

Depending on the topic you seek and the time of day, IRC channels can be very crowded, chaotic, or calm. If you hit a busy time, it can take awhile to get connected. One nice thing about the program is that if you are kicked off one channel, it will usually automatically search and try another.

Some channels are open to everyone, but others are private and open only to friends. On large IRC networks as many as twenty thousand channels may exist, while on smaller networks, there will be fewer channels.

Tips on Using IRC

If you decide to try chat, I definitely recommend lurking before you leap. Once you decide to get in on the action, here are a few answers to common questions:

→ **What is the "/" sign in chat?** Anything preceded by a slash ("/") in chat is a command for the system. Anything without a slash is assumed to be a message on chat, and will either appear on the channel window or in a private chat room where you are speaking. (Other commands are listed in the mIRC help file.)

→ **How do you join a chat room or channel?** This is simple. If you want to join, simply click right on the channel or type a command. If you want to try out commands, this is a good place to start. Find the channel's title bar and note the name, then type: "/join#(fill in the channel name here)."As a beginner, go for rooms that look hospitable. These may include "/join#irchelp" or "/join#mirc" or "/join#beginner" or anything that looks friendly to you, the newbie.

→ **Do names mean anything when it comes to chat rooms?** Simply put, no. Save for the newbie type indicators listed above, most have nothing to do with what's going on inside. A channel named #Twight_Zone, for example, may have nothing whatever to do with the TV show. For this reason—as well as many others—parents need to be sure to navigate a child's selection of chat rooms.

→ **How do I know who else is in the chat room?** To find your fellow chatters, look to the right of the channel window that will open when you first join the group. Everyone online at that time will be listed by their nickname in alphabetical order.

→ **Why do some names have a "@" beside them?** People with an "@"before their names are channel operators, who have control over a specific room or channel. Usually the operator designation is given to the first person in the room. Operators are the 'rulers' of the room. (This means that they can kick you out for pretty much any reason. If you don't like it, you're free to complain, or to start your own room. Nobody said this was democratic...)

→ **When I'm ready to talk, how do I start?** To start talking, type. When you're finished, hit the return key and watch your message join the fray.

A list of upcoming chat topics on the Yahooligans! Discussions.

No Adults Allowed!

Headbone Zone ....**www.headbone.com**
Kids and teen rooms, including a game room and a role-playing room. Registration is required, and kids who break the rules (swearing, inappropriate behavior, or giving out personal information) can be banned for up to 720 minutes.

Humongous Sports ....**www.humongoussports.com**
Sports talk for kids. Registered kids can ask questions or talk to a behind-the-scenes coach.

Kids Space Connection ....**www.ks-connection.com**
International bulletin board for kids' questions.

Kids World ....:......**www.kidsworld.org/kidsworld.html**
Monitored IRC chat on servers intended specifically for kids.

Kid Chatters ....**www.kidchatters.com.**
For a $2.95 fee, these rooms are monitored.

General Kid Chatting ....**www.main.nc.us/pace/chat.htm**
These rooms are not monitored, but they include protective guidelines.

Discussion Boards

Discussion or bulletin boards also provide ways for computer users to talk to one another, but unlike IRC chats, bulletin board conversations don't necessarily take place in real time. Instead, messages are left or 'posted' and you can return later to see any responses. On the Internet, Usenet provides thousands of discussion boards. You can talk about everything from topics as mundane as soot damage at the Homeowners Soot Damage discussion board to violin music at The Violinist board.

When it comes to kids, boards have a few advantages over immediate talk channels. Many, if not all, are built around specific topics, which means that most people on message boards are there to discuss similar concerns or interests (less chance of off-topic, or off-color, comments). Messages posted on a board are also often time-delayed—unlike IRC chat where what you type is what you see. Depending on the operators, it can take up to four hours before a message is actually posted on a board. This makes discussion safer for kids, since moderators have time to weed out inappropriate materials.

Another plus is that messages posted online in discussion board format stay up for a period of time, so lots of people get a chance to respond to questions or comments. Also, most boards are "archived" so that past discussions are saved (a great resource for—among others—the soot damaged).

Boards can be found all over the Web. One great area is About.com (**www.about.com**) where resident experts offer advice and information on everything from archery to zoology. Each site topic offers boards where interested readers can discuss the subject with the expert and other readers. Some of the best boards on About.com cover issues related to the Internet—how to design Web pages, Internet safety, and even basic programming.

Instant Messaging

Every night, between dinner, homework, and sax practice, my older son heads for his computer, not necessarily to start homework, but to begin "instant messaging," the high-tech communication practiced by millions of teens and preteens. Less intimate than a phone call, but more intimate than traditional e-mail or regular 'chat rooms,' instant messaging (IM) has clearly taken hold of teenage communication.

What is instant messaging? With an online connection and free software, a computer user types messages that instantly pop up on another chatter's screen. By opening several IM windows at once, you can have several conversations at the same time. Perhaps the biggest consumers of chat are teens, who often keep buddy lists of over a hundred friends. (For much more on IM and teen use, see Chapter 9, Teens Online.)

A Little History of Chat

Originally written by a Finnish programmer named Jarkko Oikarinen in 1988, IRC protocol didn't really take off until 1991, when Gulf War updates from around the world kept people glued to their computers and IRC channels as they followed the latest bulletins. IRC also served as a way for military personnel to keep in contact with family members during that war.

Kids' Chat and Discussion Groups

To keep kids safe online, look for chat rooms or bulletin boards that require registration and parental permission for children below age 13, and look for monitored boards that will ban kids who behave inappropriately or give out personal information. One of the best of these is KidLink chat **www.kidlink.org**, a site that contains an IRC monitored by adults and educators. Others are the sites run by Cyberkids and Cyberteens at **www.cyberkids.com**. Both Web pages offer immediate connections via Java applets from their sites.

KidLink also makes some of the best use for IRC chat when it comes to kids. Noah and I are dying to try "Who Am I?", an eight month program that lets kids explore subjects like "Where do I Live?", "What are My Rights?" and "What are My Roots?" using the Web, e-mail, and chat. Cyberteens also hosts a number of well-thoughtout topic boards, including music and favorite reads.

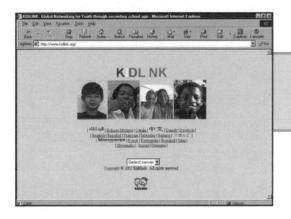

Kidlink offers a great IRC chat for kid-based discussions.

Chat Tips

If any area of the Internet has gotten bad press over the years, it's been chat and chat rooms. And there is some reason for parental concern. In a 2001 study reported in *The Journal of the American Medical Association*, twenty percent—one out of five—of regular Internet users between the ages of 10 and 17 said they had received at least one unwanted sexual advance online. Stories about child predators online, kids succumbing to invitations to meet strangers, children wandering into inappropriate chat rooms, be they violent or sexual, have been all too common in the national press.

The truth is that if taken as a percentage, compared to the number of kids online, these cases are rare. But despite their infrequency, the stories are tragic and, without doubt, scary.

So how much should your worry?

"Quite frankly, the risk of Instant Messaging and e-mail have been exaggerated," says Steven Jones, Ph.D, Professor of Communications at the University of Illinois in Chicago. "Kids are pretty smart, and most of them are aware of dangers. If they've been taught well not to engage with strangers in the world, they can deal with strangers online."

Jones sees the parental panic as a familiar response to new technology, not unknown at the start of the century with film or television. "The Internet hasn't been around very long. It's threatening because it invades a private space of the home. But the sky isn't falling. Parents simply need to school their kids to be careful."

Although parents should keep a keen eye on all of kids' Internet use, it's particularly important to set out a clear policy with your kids when it comes to chat rooms. Because many chat rooms deal with adult material, young children should never explore these sites without parental supervision or prior permission to go onto a specific channel or bulletin board, preferably one that is limited to kids only. Remind your kids never to give private information out online—including their real names, e-mail address, age, phone number, school or home address—and never to agree to meet face-to-face with any strangers they meet online. No matter how friendly or sympathetic the person may appear, remind your kids that people they meet on the Internet are not always what they seem to be.

Other tips:

→ **Chat rooms are sometimes organized around topics.** Warn your kids to avoid topic areas or conversations that make them uncomfortable.

→ **Be especially careful** of chat rooms that get into subjects that might be associated with sex or cults or groups that practice potentially dangerous rituals.

→ **Even when rooms are labeled "kids only"' others may sneak on board.** Remember that not everyone is what they present themselves to be. Stay on guard.

→ Be **suspicious** of anyone who tries to turn you against your parents, teachers, or friends. They may have a **hidden agenda**.

→ On some services and Web sites you can enter into a **private chat area** where you can arrange to meet friends. In some cases, those rooms are truly private. But in other cases, they may be listed in a directory of rooms. If so, there is nothing to stop others from entering those rooms. Also, don't go into a private area if you don't feel comfortable doing so.

→ To **avoid online harassment**, have your kids choose a gender-neutral name— like initials or a word—to use in a chat room. It's fine to be cute or funny with the name you choose, but make sure it doesn't identify you and doesn't have any meaning or implication that might encourage others to bother you.

→ **Intruders** in "kids- or teens-only" chat rooms should be reported to the server or Internet Provider.

Build Your Own
Web
Page

Chapter 5

Build Your Own Web Page

Sooner or later, your child will pose the question every Internet-connected parent must eventually face: "Where do Web sites come from?" And while you fumble around to change the subject, "Can we make our own?"

Before you offer to explain the facts of life or give him a baby sister if he'll just forget about that durned Web stuff, I'm here to tell you to take heart. Despite what you may have heard, creating your own Web page is pretty much, well, child's play.

The trick here is to think less about the technical difficulties ahead (we'll get you through those) and more about the creative and educational opportunities. And according to experts like Idit Harel, founder of the interactive children's Web site MaMaMedia.com, children, like adults, learn best by doing.

"Making their own Web pages gives kids a great chance to actively connect to a project," she says. "And even better, when they finish, they get to share it with the world online."

Once you think about it on Harel's terms, Web design and making a Web site become the modern kid's equivalent of crayoning, painting, pasting, and cartooning all in one. (All this and no mess to clean up!)

We'll save the facts of life for another day.

Get Animated

Kaleidoscape's Kid Place **www.kaleidoscapes.com/kidsplace/index.html**
Free tutorials on how to do online animation, plus a WYSIWYG editor and two week storage space for your own animated page.

The Challenge: Paging Us!

Ready, Set, Type...

Noah and I face our first Web page with a bit of trepidation. After all, we weren't talking about posting artwork on the refrigerator door. To prepare ourselves, we decided to take a critical tour of the Web, to get a sense of what else was out there, and maybe to pick up a few hints on color, composition, and design. As we looked, we talked about what we liked—and disliked—about different sites and tried to answer our many, many questions:

→ Who did we want to visit our page?

→ Did we want it to be a kids' page?

→ Should we let people e-mail comments to us?

→ What colors worked well together?

→ Which type faces were easy to read? Which weren't?

→ How much information was too much?

→ Did we want to have advertisements on our site?

Before you embark on making your first site, you might want to conduct a similar search. Once you've considered some of the design and audience elements, move onto content. Do you have a favorite sport or a team you want to celebrate? Do you keep a diary that you want to share? (Lots of teenagers do this.) Does your family have an interesting history? Do you have a prize rooster? Or cat? You can promote your favorite ice cream recipes, your home grown poetry, or an excellent collection of ancient sneakers, or...well, look around, you'll be amazed at the things people put up on the web.

All of this preliminary footwork will help you decide what belongs on your site and what doesn't. For example, does that adorable picture of your goldfish Sparky really belong on a page devoted to your favorite ice hockey team? It also will help you decide on your target audience: i.e. who do you want to visit your pages? A 9-year-old's page dedicated to his love of Bart Simpson will be considerably different in design, content, and tone than a 16-year-old's tribute to John Coltrane, or one made by a grandmother, eager to brag about the accomplishments of her grandchildren.

While you're on the prowl for ideas, it's also good to consider—in a larger sense—what you want to accomplish with your production. Are you out to entertain, educate, or gross out potential visitors? Entertainment sites probably will require more updates so that people will keep returning to see what's new. Educational or reference sites that reflect an interest—pages on all you ever wanted to know about goldfish (Go, Sparky!) or planting sunflowers—can draw hobbyists or novices eager for information. And gross sites—well, we'll let you figure that out for yourself.

Love at First Site: HTML or WYSIWYG?

Once you've given some thought to what you want to have on your page, all you have to do is build it. Here again, you have a choice. You can code your page using HTML—a language that describes your page so that a browser can interpret it, or you can use a Web Editor, fondly called a WYSIWYG (wiz-ee-wig) or What You See Is What You Get editor, since the document will print just like it appears on the computer monitor. An HTML WYSIWYG editor will simply present design elements to you, and you can drag or click them until you see the page of your dreams. Or, if you want to get really fancy, you can employ HTML code to improve your WYSIWYG design.

Enough alphabet soup, let's get designing.

Style Check

A number of sites around the Web are geared to help the novice Web page designer. Several address issues for the beginner, while others take you to the next level in evaluating and experimenting with design. Easy to understand articles on everything from basic authoring of Web sites to advanced Web design can be found at Webmonkey (**http://hotwired.lycos.com/webmonkey**).

An entire course on principles of typography, Web graphics and more, produced by Yale University is available at **http://info.med.yale.edu/caim/manual**.

Web Page Design for Designers offers advanced tips on making the most of a Web page. Not for beginners, but check out the page's own excellent use of type and color for ideas. See **www.wpdfd.com/**.

Hypertext Markup Language

In the old days, most people used HTML (HyperText Markup Language) to create Web sites. HTML is a language of markup symbols or codes that tells your Web browser how to display a Web pages' words and images. Each individual markup code is referred to as an element or tag.

To see the HTML elements that make up a Web page, pick a page, any page. Noah suggested the New York Mets fan page—the site of our favorite, though often frustrating, baseball team. Using the Microsoft Internet Explorer browser, we right-clicked on a blank area of the page to get a menu and clicked Source. You can also go to View on the toolbar to find the Source command. With a click, a notepad popped up covered with HTML tags that describe the site.

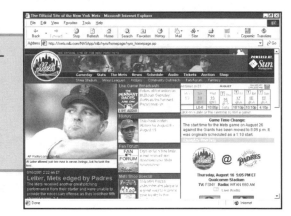

Right-Click anywhere on the Mets page to bring up the 'view source' tool.

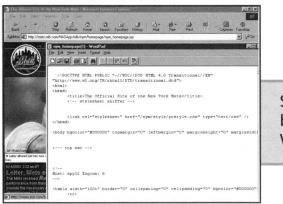

Source code: the bare bones of a Web page in HTML.

Although we love the Mets (I know, don't send mail to the publisher), even we have to admit this notepad made us nervous. But before you run off to use a Web Editor, know that HTML isn't that tough. Mainly, it's cumbersome. You can't see what will be on the page without clicking back and forth between the preview of the finished product and the HTML notepad. And it involves a lot of pesky code, which you have to keep referring back to as you work.

Yet there are good reasons to know a little HTML, even if you plan to use a Web Editor to build your page. Sometimes, even the best editors can make mistakes, and if you're going after a certain effect, you can click into the source code and adjust it with HTML. This may seem a bit scary, but hey, who ever thought you'd be doing your own page in the first place?

Not us. So, here are a few words on HTML.

→ **HTML elements are called tags.** They are surrounded by angle brackets "<>" and almost always travel in pairs. Code can be written in lower or upper case—it doesn't matter.

→ **The first tag usually turns the action on;** the second shuts it off. The second tag—the shut off—is preceded by a forward slash. For example, if you want a word to be in bold, precede it by <B>. When you're ready to return to a regular font, simply close the passage with </B>.

→ **Tags can be imbedded in other tags.** When this occurs, you need to open and close tags in order. This, for example, is wrong: <head><title> My Web Page! </head></title>. The right way: <head><title> My Web Page</title></head>.

→ **All HTML pages** begin with <html> and end with </html>.

→ **Everything that will appear** on screen is included in the <body> </body> tags.

For our first attempt, I set Mr. Noah loose. In Microsoft Internet Explorer, click the Start button, scroll to Accessories, then hit Notepad. Noah then writes his code:

```
<html>
<head><title>Noah's Totally Awesome HTML Web Page
</title></head>
<body>This is so cool. Mom will never understand how it works</body>
</html>
```

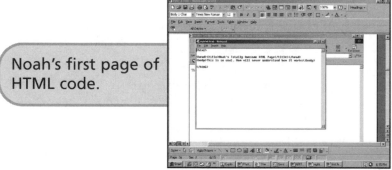

Noah's first page of HTML code.

He saves it as an HTML file: Myhtml.html.

Now let's move to the fun part. Once it's saved, we go onto the browser, and open up the file. This is what the browser produced.

Notice where the code sends his message—the title is the title of the page. His URL is the name of the saved file of code: myhtml.html.

The body of the message is a false, poorly punctuated statement. Mom has figured out how this works, more or less.

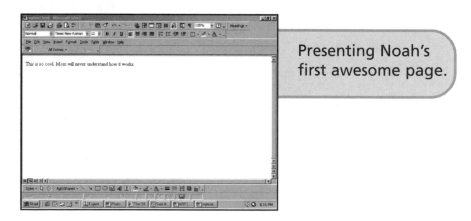

Presenting Noah's first awesome page.

More HTML

Of course, there's plenty more to learn about HTML—adding type fonts, shrinking and enlarging copy, color, images, you name it. The best place to learn more about HTML is literally at your fingertips. The Web holds a huge number of tutorials—presented by companies, computer magazines, and the occasional 13-year-old boy or girl—available either for free in freeware or in shareware for a minimal price.

Once you get the hang of the basic page design, you'll be ready for some fancy stuff. The first place to head for the mother lode of information about HTML is the W3C's (World Wide Web Consortium's) Recommendation for HTML. While everything you ever wanted to learn about HTML appears on their excellent site, most of it can be pretty heavy lifting. For less technical advice, go for columns written by Dave Raggett, an HTML wizard. Begin with "Getting Started with HTML" (www.w3.org/MarkUp/Guide/).

Some Basic HTML Tags

Structure Tags

These tags set up the format of the page.

HTML: <html> begins the document file; </html> ends the file.

Head: <head> begins the header; </head> closes the header.

Title: <title> begins the title of the document; </title> closes it.

Body: <body> begins the body of the document; </body> closes it.

Background color: Add bgcolor = "color" (you pick the color, e.g. "green") within the <body> tag. For example, <body bgcolor= "green">

Center: Text and graphics are left-justified when displayed in your browser, but if you want to "center" portions of your page, use the <center> tag.

Comments: <--begins comments that will not appear on the page--> closes them.

These are used for remarks that won't be read by the browser, such as information for the designer about page elements, or details about your page that can be read by search engine 'bots and spiders instead of meta tags.

Text Tags

These tags change the size, appearance, and color of your text.

Big: `<big>`makes words larger; `</big>` closes it.

Small: `<small>` makes words smaller; `</small>` closes it.

Bold: `<b>` creates a bold font; `</b>` closes it.

Emphasize: `<em>` puts emphasis, usually by italicizing words, though users can adjust their browsers to control how it displays 'emphasized' text;`</em>` closes it.

Italicize: `<i>` creates italicized text; `</i>`closes it.

Underline: `<u>`creates underlined text; `</u>`closes it.

Breaks: Browsers need instructions to make carriage returns, tabs, and extra spaces:

`<br>` creates a line break; no close.

`<p>` makes a paragraph break; no close.

Font: Increase font sizes of your text with `<font></font>`. Increase font by step sizes:`<font size=+1>....</font>` From 1 to 7.

Change font color: `<font color= "color">... "color"</font>`. (Insert color of your choice, e.g. `<font color="blue">blue</font>`. Try lights and darks, such as "lightblue."

Headings: `<h1>` creates a heading; `</h1>` closes it. (Headings run in descending size from `<h1>` to `<h6>`.)

Link Tags

These tags link phrases or images in your file to the WWW.

Add a link: use `<a>` tags to create a link to another Web page or to allow visitors to e-mail you from your site.

To add a Web page link:

`<a href=http://www.marspub.com/>Mars Publishing</a>`

This will show up on your page as <u>Mars Publishing</u>, and clicking it will open Mars Publishing's website.

To create a link with your e-mail address:

`<a href="mailto: ilene.raymond@marspub.com">Author</a>`

Looks like this, <u>Author</u>, and addresses an e-mail to me.

Image Tags

It's easy to insert an image onto your page. Images can be created by a digital camera, by scanning an image in, or creating one with a painting or drawing program.

Image: <img src=> "image file" width="number of pixels" height = "number of pixels"; no close.

How does this work? Let's say you have an image file called "MyGoldfishSparky.jpg." To add the image:

1. Save it in the same folder/directory as your HTML file so your browser can find it. It is 200 pixels wide by 150 pixels high.

2. Type in <img src="MyGoldfishSparky.jpg" width="200" height="150">

3. Add a short description to help people identify the picture.

<img src="MyGoldfishSparky.jpg" width="200" height="150" alt= "yellow fish in a bowl">

Note: Web page image files should be either GIF or JPG files. All images have one of these two extensions, so if you have an image "pal," it will be labeled either "pal.gif" or "pal.jpg."

List tags

You can create three types of lists: unordered, ordered, and descriptive.

Unordered: Unordered lists look like this:

* apples

* oranges

* peaches

To get this effect start with <ul>, and tag <li> (short for list item) before each item on the list. Close with </ul>.

<ul>
<li>apples
<li>oranges
<li>peaches
</ul>

Ordered list: Ordered lists show items in a logical, numbered order.

   Adam

   Betsy

   Carl

To achieve this numerical list, use the tags <ol> to start, itemize each element with <li> and close with </ol>. Use the format for theunordered list shown above.

If you want to change how you're organizing your ordered list, add a "type" designation within the <ol> tag. For example:

<ol type= "A"> orders the list by capital letters:(A, B, C…)

<ol type = "I"> orders the list by Roman numerals: (I, II, III…)

Descriptive list: This shows a list of text items with an indented second line.
Big Muckety Muck

   Super Famous Corporation

Second in Command

   Super Famous Corporation

Use the following tags:

```
<dl>
<dt>Big Muckety Muck
<dd>Super Famous Corporation
<dt>Second in Command
<dd>Super Famous Corporation
</dl>
```

Meta Tags

No matter how you decide to promote your site, you'll have the most luck (and more hits) with a specific title page and a good description of your site that clearly depicts the contents.

To gather information, some bots—those robots that scan Web sites for their search engine database—read Meta tags. Meta tags can be inserted in the heading area of your page.

Let's promote our page, "Where in the World Are Mom & Noah?" To start with, this isn't really a great title because it doesn't actually describe the contents specifically. After a little brainstorming, we came up with "Keyboard Explorers," a bit more catchy and a bit more to the point. If you're using HTML, the top of the page might look something like this:

```
<html>
<head>
<title>Keyboard Explorers </title>
```

Now, once you set that up, you need to give the bot something to look at: a picture of your page. It's time to use a comment:

```
<!—Go on an exciting armchair tour of the globe with
a mother and son who love to explore the world via the
Internet. Travel with us.—!>
```

That should give search engines that don't use meta tags enough working material. For engines that use meta tags, however, you need to add another two lines beneath the commentary entry. The first meta tag will describe your site; the second will provide "keywords" to help bots to categorize your entry.

```
<html>
<head>
<title>Keyboard Travelers</title>
<! —Explore the globe without leaving your keyboard.
Mother-son travel guides take you on a wild and bumpy ride
around our home planet —>
META name= "description" Content = "Explore the globe
without leaving your keyboard. Mother-son travel guides
take you on a wild and bumpy ride around our home
planet."
META name = "keywords" Content = "TRAVEL, TRAVELLERS,
KEYBOARD, GLOBE, MOTHER, SON, GUIDES, PLANET."
</head>
```

On the search engine, your entry will appear something like this:
Keyboard Travelers

Explore the globe without leaving your keyboard. Mother-son travel guides take you on a wild and bumpy ride around our home planet. **www.noahandmom.homestead.com/noahandmom.com.html**

Not every search engine supports meta tags. Two that do are Excite and AltaVista. (For a short tutorial that will help you set up tags see **www.excite.com/info/getting_listed/meta_tags**).

Special Effects

Once you become a Web builder, you're probably going to start looking at the Web in a new way. At least we did. Pre-making-our-own-pages, Noah and I might see something like falling confetti or bouncing balls or a Java applet that popped up in the center of the screen to show us a hamster doing his daily constitutional and say, "Awesome." Post-making-our-own-site, we're apt to say, "How did they do that?"

This is where knowing a little bit of HTML can help. Even if you are using a Web Editor, you can open your page and add HTML to get special effects. To get a few of these applications (the Web's version of an HTML cheat sheet), go to the sites below to find answers to some of the great mysteries:

→ How do you float balloons down a page? Head for **www.dynamicdrive.com/dynamicindex4/flyimage.htm**, where all will be revealed.

→ How do you get little images to follow your cursor? Follow them to **www.dynamicdrive.com/dynamicindex4/trailer.htm**

→ How do you get little snowflakes to drop all over your site? Go for **www.dynamicdrive.com/dynamicindex3/snow.htm**.

→ How about autumn leaves? They're dropping at **www.dynamicdrive.com/dynamicindex3/leaves.htm**

→ And last but not least, a butterfly… **www.dynamicdrive.com/dynamicindex4/butterfly.htm**

Cool Tools to Check Your HTML

When editing HTML, it's easy to make mistakes. Wouldn't it be nice if there was a simple way to fix these mistakes automatically and tidy up sloppy editing into nicely laid out markup? Dave Raggett's HTML TIDY is a free utility for doing just that. Tidy is able to fix up a wide range of problems and to bring to your attention things that you need to work on yourself.

Each item found is listed with the line number and column so that you can see where the problem lies in your markup. Tidy won't generate a cleaned up version when there are problems that it can't be sure how to handle. These are logged as "errors" rather than "warnings." For more see, **www.w3.org/People/Raggett/tidy/**

A second service provided via the W3C (The World Wide Web Consortium) is an HTML Validator. This checks your HTML code to see if it complies with organizational standards. See **http://validator.w3.org/**

Web Editors or WYSIWYGs

After fooling around with HTML a little, you might realize it has a few limitations. One, you can't see the elements you're putting in without clicking back and forth from the notepad to the page. Secondly, it's terrifically time consuming.

Web Page Editors to the rescue. A WYSIWYG (wiz-ee-wig) editor or program is one that allows you to design the Web page so you can see what the end result will look like while you're creating it. There are a number on the Web offered either as freeware or shareware.

If you're working with Netscape or Microsoft browsers, you can go to your browser home page, where you can find an editor. But there are many other options on the Web, several designed especially for kids (and beginners) that are, frankly, shamefully easy to use. As absolute startups exhausted by our foray into HTML, Noah and I were primed for Hot Dog Junior.

To repeat: Hot Dog Junior is a very, very basic program that can be used by a seven year old. A great green cartoon dog offers options, including art, design, and background, which you can practice on. Without purchasing the software ($39.95 at the time this was written), you can't upload your page onto the Internet from the site, but you can download the program easily and begin practicing your design skills and get a feel for what you want to put on your page. (Download from a great download site at Tucows.com, **www.tucows.com/preview/194531.html**)

The Hot Dog Junior Editor sets out four basic steps to making your Web page: Choose Your Page (where you pick a template), Build Your Page (here's where the meat is: links, images, heading, and so on), View Your Page (in Hot Dog Jr. or using your browser), and Upload Your Page (to the server you plan to run the page from).

Working with Hot Dog Junior turned out to be a snap. In less than fifteen minutes, Noah had picked out his Top Secret theme, along with a secret password puzzle for me to guess at. (Hint: an oinker smells with it).

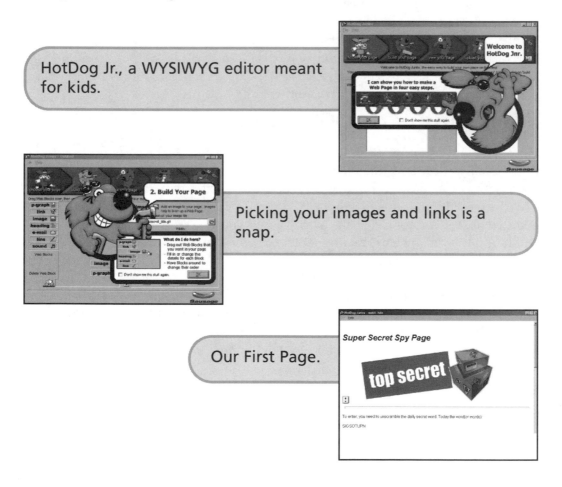

HotDog Jr., a WYSIWYG editor meant for kids.

Picking your images and links is a snap.

Our First Page.

A number of other, slightly more complex WYSIWIG editors can also be downloaded as freeware or shareware from the Web. Most of these include site builder programs that permit you to click options from a list of possible typestyles, colors, or graphic effects or click and drag options that let you pull design options right onto your site. Many also offer templates that help you to plan your site.

Flush with the victory of creating two whole pages, Noah and I went to **www.homestead.com** to try out their Web page builder. For a small monthly fee, this site offers a site builder and storage space for your masterpiece. A Java applet program you install onsite, called Homestead Homebuilder, offers all sorts of tempting special effects. (So many special effects, so little time!)

For this creation, we arrived with a high concept: to share our love of travel with the world. We went with the theme of "Where in the World Are Noah and Mom?"

Clicking into the site, we selected a personal Web page option, then loaded a Java applet that makes design a question of clicking and dragging elements around the screen. Options included a background wallpaper (we picked purple), different color type styles, and a number of add-ons, like links to the popular auction house e-bay, e-mail connections, and a counter that would let us know how many people have visited our site.

Once we had finished, we previewed our creation. Granted, we had probably violated a number of good design principles, but it had been fun. I was pleased, but Noah gave it a critical eye.

"It doesn't do anything," he complained.

After a little thought, we decided that we should link our site to pages that had something to do with places: a sort of travel-portal for armchair voyagers. Among the links we added (a simple matter of clicking onto a menu, inserting the URL of the connecting site, and the deed was done) were **www.greatestplaces.org**, a geography site that offers games, maps to whet any living room traveler's appetite, and **www.nationalgeographic.com/geobee**, a site that offers info, maps, and games on geography.

To make the links appear less naked, we put buttons on top of the links, so that a visitor could simply hit the suitcase and speed on.

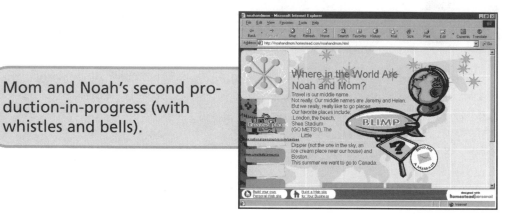

Mom and Noah's second pro-duction-in-progress (with whistles and bells).

Adding links to our page with the homebuilder at Homestead.com.

Web Pages for Kids (**www.diall.net/webpagesforkids/**) and Kids on the Web (**www.diall.net/webpagesforkids/**) both offer terrific, easy to understand explanations on creating Web pages for kids and teens. (Adults might like them, too.)

If you want the convenience of a site builder and design help and a place to get your file on the Internet for free, we can also recommend http://geocities.yahoo.com/ and www.angelfire.com. Both offer a variety of graphics and some very good design help for the artistically challenged. Along with tutorials on how to make Web sites, both of these sites offer a long list of add-ons to personalize your page and to keep visitors coming back for more. Among them: stock quotes, weather reports, maps, a counter (to keep track of your visitors) and on the Yahoo! Site—a Web cam.

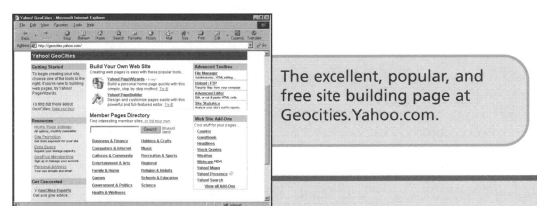

The excellent, popular, and free site building page at Geocities.Yahoo.com.

Hands-On HTML

Interested in exploring HTML? You've come to the right place. The Web is bursting with places to perfect your HTML building skills. To start, take a look at an interesting library of HTML only templates at **www.angelfire.com/doc/htmllib/**. Click View, then source, and study the codes. While you can do this with any page on the Web, many incorporate fancier languages that might confuse the HTML beginner.

Check out Internet Primer (**http://archive.ncsa.uiuc.edu/General/Internet/WWW/HTMLPrimer.html**) —a great resource for basic HTML. Best for older kids (and their parents), grades 9 through 12.

Written by a sixth grader, Lissa Explains All at **www.lissaexplains.com/** not only has great basics, but additional fun stuff to add color and pizzazz to your page. To learn "How Web Pages Work" head for the clear explanation on **www.howstuffworks.com**. In addition to taking you through the mysteries of HTML, the site offers a little pretend notepad to practice your skills, and a one page reference of HTML tags. Everything you wanted to know about HTML plus Web page publishing can be found at WEBAlley **www.weballey.net/html/software.html**. The site leans heavily to HTML as the way to design Web sites. To find tags quickly, explore **www.zdnet.com/devhead/resources/tag_library/**, a dictionary of HTML. Simply hit a letter and get an entire list of command codes.

Clip Art

Since the Web is a visual medium, you're going to want to import images to your site. Web Page Editors contain art to simply click or click and drag onto your site. But if you want to step out, there are many sites where free art can be found. If you're using a WYSIWYG, you can follow instructions to import gif files onto your page. Or go to **www.buttonmaker.com** where you can find a free tool to bring animation or clip art to your pride and joy.

Art is all over the Web. The one caveat: pay attention to the copyright provisions. Some sites want you to credit art; others want a minimal fee. Among the many:

➜ Feeling animated? Head towards the Animation Factory (**http://animfactory.com**) and check out over 15,000 free animated figures waiting to spice up your pages.

➜ Kids' Domain Art (**www.kidsdomain.com**) covers holidays: Mother's Day, Father's Day, and Adopt-a-Stuffed Animal Day.

➜ DisneyClipart!! (**http://disneyclipart.com**) contains over 1500 familiar cartoon images.

➜ Yahoo! Picture Gallery (**http://gallery.yahoo.com**) offers photos from sports, nature, and geography. (We're planning to add them to "Where in the World Are Noah and Mom?" once we find some space.)

➜ Cool Archives (**www.coolarchive.com**) contains everything you need from buttons to HTML tips to backgrounds and much more.

Solid Web Tips

While Noah and I were artistically fulfilled by "Where in the World Are Mom and Noah?" we'd be willing to admit it's a little, well, busy. And a mite hard to read. Two things that you don't want people to say about your Web page. While you're welcome to fool around and no one is knocking the value of personal expression, it's good to know a few basics of good design. (Less is more...)

→ **Before you start building a site, take a pencil and make a few sketches of what you're after.** Block in where images and text will appear. Do you want to link to other sites? Do you want your title to appear flush to the left or center? Will your links be underlined, in a different color than the rest of the type, or both?

→ **Friendly is best.** Make a good first impression with warm colors, easy to read fonts, and clear presentations—particularly on your home page.

→ **What's in a name?** A sense of mystery and intrigue about your URL name will lead people to your site. My Cat Page or Danny's Baseball Site are less intriguing than Felines on the Prowl! or Strike Four. Use your imagination to draw people in.

→ **Less is more.** Blinking displays, changing colors, and loads of graphics are great, but if you overdo it, visitors may feel overcharged and simply click on. Also, more stuff means longer loading times. (A good tip from a Zen Web designer: hold your breath as your finished site begins loading. If you expire before the page comes up, chances are good you need to do some fine tuning.)

→ **Choose color wisely.** Colors that have something to do with your subject are best. To avoid busyness and reduce eyestrain, avoid using all 216 colors available (at least at the same time).

→ **Check readability.** Three points here: pick type fonts that you can read without trouble, try to put them on a background that keeps them legible, and use blocks of type. When it comes to Web design, four sentences in a block of type, with white space in the margins and in between blocks, ups the chances that your audience will get your message. Black type on white backgrounds remains the most boring, but also the most legible. This is one area where checking other pages can help. If you can't read fuchsia on hot purple bricks, chances are no one else can, either.

→ **Use a spellchecker.** Need I say more?

→ **Proofread your work.** Then do it again. Sending up a page on the Internet means exposing yourself—literally—to the world. Check to make sure your links work and that your graphics load correctly.

→ **Keep your site up to date.** By regularly changing your site, updating links and adding new features, you'll encourage people to come back to your site often to see what's new. There's nothing worse than returning to the site and finding outdated links.

→ **Put in a site map.** You can download free software to do this from www.coffeecup.com. It's called an Image Map maker and can help you plug in different pages in an organized way for your site.

Web Page Editors

Angelfire ....**http://angelfire.lycos.com**
Arachnophia ....**www.arachnoid.com/arachnophilia**
Cool Page ....**www.coolpage.com**
CuteHTML ....**www.globalscape.com/products/cutehtml/index.shtml**
FrontPage ....**www.microsoft.com/frontpage**
Homestead ....**www.homestead.com**
HoTMetal Pro............**www.hotmetalpro.com**
Layout Master ....**www.westciv.com/layout_master**
Namo Web................**www.namo.com**
Site Aid ....**www.amiasoft.com/siteaid/PageSpinner**

Showing Off Your Site

Whether you opt to build with a WYSIWYG or HTML, once you finish, you're going to want to show it off.

Unlike other artistic creations, which might be private or, at best, refrigerator magnet worthy, Web pages are meant to be seen (and, if you have the equipment, heard). So when you're done, you'll need a way—preferably free—to eventually get your pages uploaded for the masses to visit.

Unless you sign up with an online community that offers Web pages that can be shown right from their site, you'll need an FTP client. FTP stands for File Transfer Protocol and that's what it does: transfer files from one computer to another. In this case it will transfer your file from your computer to the server of the company you signed up with to host your page.

When you sign up with someone to host your page, they will give you info that you put into the appropriate places in your FTP client. Click connect and you're there. Once plugged into their server, you can send files over and later, if you need to, copy them right back to your computer.

So, if you want to go the FTP route, your first step will be to contact your Internet Service Provider to see if they host free space. If they don't, or, if you don't mind joining an Internet community—which means filling out a few forms to get an account and an identifying password—you can get free space at several (laces online. To get started, you might want to check out free-space-offered communities such as Angel fire (**www.angelfire.com**), Tripod (**www.tripod.lycos.com**), and Yahoo!

Once your site is up and running, you can get it onto search engines and directories. Go to Yahoo! where a Frequently Asked Question (FAQ) page is available to help you categorize your file. Personal pages are listed in the 'Society & Culture' sections. AltaVista offers a direct link where you submit your URL into the search engine.

Projects: Webbing It

→ **Play with HTML:** Although you might not want to use HTML to design an entire Web page, it's fun (and powerful) to play with it a little. Practice using color and importing images.

→ **Do you Blog?:** Web sites come in all kinds of varieties and flavors, including online diaries. The word diary is a bit tricky since many "bloggers" not only report on their own daily doings but scour the Web for great sites that they link onto their own. Read all about them at **www.blogger.com**, then, when you're fired up, get started on your very own blog for free at The Blog Spot **www.blogspot.com** or **www.bloghop.com**.

→ **You don't like our Stinky Hamster Web Page?** We love our idea for our next project: stinky hamsters. But if you want to branch out into some new areas, Webmonkey has some great projects that give you practice in design elements of HTML. Included are making your own (or someone else's) birthday invitation, experimenting with colors, and creating a self-portrait with a digital camera. All of the projects involve developing skills that can be applied to improving a Web page or two. They also have clear directions for parents and teachers who are along for the ride. Pedal over to **http://hotwired.lycos.com/webmonkey/kids/projects/index.html**.

→ **Still fishing for Ideas?** For examples of parent & child pages made with HTML, go to **www.kent.wednet.edu/staff/hbuchwal/kidsparents**. Don't forget to check the source code. Is it time to invest in a digital camera?

Playing Around

Chapter 6

Playing Around

It's 7:00 a.m. on a Sunday morning, and Noah has corralled me from bed to sit before the trusty PC to help him play his latest obsession—online Boggle. Unbelievably enough, there are eight other lost souls out there in the world who have also started their day with a brain challenging test to find as many over three-letter words as they can in three-minutes.

Noah is under the perfectly acceptable but totally erroneous illusion that Mom the Writer will be good at this game. And though I haven't yet had my morning cup of Java, I am a pretty fair player. I watch the seconds tick down, fingers flying over the keys, egged on by Noah's cheers. In his mind, I will finally boost his 774 score to the heavens.

Three for the Keyboard

Familiar Favorites: Apart from Boggle, the Net offers a number of family friendly and familiar games, including checkers, chess and Battleship. Play checkers against a computer at **www.darkfish.com/checkers/Checkers2.html** or Battleship at **www.head-crash.com/battle.**

Calling all Card Sharks: Bridge, Pinochle, Go Fish or whatever else makes your Hearts stir can be found online. Play with partners or interactively with players from around the globe. Noah and I have enjoyed plenty of time around **www.solitairenetwork.com.**

Board games: Six versions of mancala, backgammon, 22 variants of Othello, and 14 versions of tic-tac-toe of varying complexity can be found at Mind Sports World Wide (**www.msoworld.com/playgames.html**).

And then the time is up and we see, somehow, that out of the eight players online, we are ranked eighth. Noah's score plummets forty some points. The players congratulate one another (the winning players, that is), and the clock restarts.

"This time, Mom," says my loyal, deluded child.

Two minutes and thirty seconds, one minute and ten, 45 seconds and then, blip, time's up and somehow—even I cannot believe it—we are once again at the bottom of the pile. Score drops fifty points. "Tough luck," one of the more gracious victors offers.

"I thought you were good at this," he sighs.

"Winning isn't everything?"

"Humph."

Gaming online—be it Crazy Eights, Age of Empires or Bowling—can be a humbling experience. For Noah and I, Boggle remains a game, but to some of our fellow Internet gamers (like Ms. 2,673 points!), it might be a way of life.

Pick Your Brain

Fun Brain...**www.funbrain.com/brainbowl/twoplay.html**
Parent-child current event quizzes let you play against one another on weekly events. Results can be played interactively or on the same computer. Good for older kids, too.

Geography Quizzes ....**www.lizardpoint.com/fun/geoquiz/usaquiz.html**
Click on maps and get three guesses to identify where you are. A word to the wise: this can be a humbling exercise for geo-challenged parents.

Yahoo!Games..**http://games.yahoo.com**
This portal offers a wide variety of all types of online games. Try some of the fiendishly delicious word games: if you like scrabble, give spelldown a whirl.

Interactive Games: Pros and Cons

Games and kids go together like peanut butter and jelly. Traditional kids' games from stickball to playing with dolls to tag help kids develop important social and mental skills.

But computer and video games, as most parents are well aware, have garnered plenty of bad press. Interactive games have been accused of turning kids into game "addicts," encouraging misbehavior at home and at school, and even promoting violent activity.

Less well publicized are the upsides of interactive games. Played in moderation, age appropriate, well-designed games can offer kids positive chances to test (and better) their skills against those of a computer or other players. Computer games can help kids boost their strategic and critical thinking and teach them creative problem solving.

Online games also provide unique ways to play with kids from around the world from the safety and comfort of their own computer screens. This means that while your child may be playing an online soccer game in his family room in Kansas, his fellow players may include a recent Russian immigrant living in Manhattan, a surfer dude in California, and a friend down the block who is seated not beside him, but in his own living room.

So what is the bottom line on Internet games?

"It all depends on the type of game and how long a child plays at it," says Larry Rosen, Ph.D, professor of psychology at California State University, Dominquez Hills, and author of *Technostress: Coping With Technology @Work@Home@Play*. Along with his wife, Michelle Weil, Ph.D., Rosen recently released a study, "Are Computer, Video and Arcade Games Affecting Children's Behavior?" While the survey examined the influence of computer and video games connected to TV sets rather than Internet connected games, the findings can shed light on the increasing number of online interactive games.

Among the study's findings were that violent or age inappropriate games can encourage certain types of misbehavior. For some—not all—kids, this can mean becoming overly aggressive, restless, and exhibiting behavior that may mimic attention deficit disorder. Basically, Rosen found that computer games can raise stress levels for young players, which may result in an inability to focus and irritability, both of which can create learning problems in school, where activities tend to move at a slower pace.

"High powered rapid paced games put kids into a 'zone' that doesn't mimic other types of play like baseball," he says. "They get used to reacting quickly to stimuli sprayed on a screen. Life isn't this quick."

While stressing that such symptoms won't be found in every child, and that his study focused on video or handheld rather than Internet games, Rosen encourages parents to make sure that the games children play are both content and age appropriate, and to moderate their interactive game playing with other, non-tech, activities. All of which comes under the heading of "good parenting."

For some children and teens, the challenges and excitement of interactive games online can become a problem. But, as several experts note, kids who tend to become 'obsessive' about games, are also often kids who experience problems in other areas of their lives.

So how do you know when it's too much?

"Moderation is key," says Richard Sherman, Ph.D, a California clinical psychologist specializing in children and adolescents and technology issues. "If your child has trouble focusing on schoolwork, if they're isolated from other kids, or neglecting other activities, you may have a problem."

The message appears clear: if your child is spending more time on the computer than his schoolwork, if he stops calling friends and neglects other activities like reading or sports, it might be time to find out why.

Games Online

More and more games familiar to kids as computer or video games now feature, or will soon feature, interactive elements. These include "Everquest," a popular online game where players assume a role in a medieval world (including slaying dragons and other dangerous monsters). A "Star Wars" based game is also headed for the Net, as well as the best-selling "Sims," where users get to play God and control lives of onscreen characters. The recently released "Majestic"—described by its designer, Electronic Arts of Redwood City (**www.ea.com**) as an "X-Files" style mystery with monthly installments—will play out through faxes, streaming video, phone calls, and instant messages to players.

Most of these games will charge a subscription fee of about $10 per month, while some will require players to buy separate software to play. And, while many new games will first be offered on personal computers online, most will eventually be directed towards Sony PlayStations or Microsoft Xboxes.

Right now, the Internet offers a wide variety of games for the pre-school and elementary aged set, along with challenging games for teens. When it comes to traditional possibilities, our house many an hour (or three or four) has been lost to online chess (which my 16-year-old finds best of the Web board games) or to solitaire. For Mom, Tetris, Battleship, and a game called Snood has sent more than one freelance project spiraling later—and later—into the evening. And let's not forget some of Noah's new discoveries, like the Harry Potter Quidditch inspired "Broomsticks," or the silly hamster update on the old favorite, "Pong," both of which can be found at **www.surfnetkids.com**.

Try your hand at Broomsticks, a variation of Quidditch.

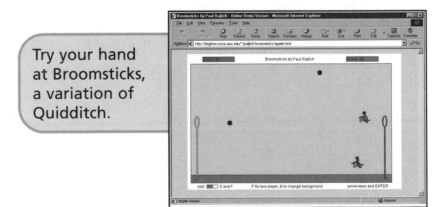

Types of Games Online

Games offered online run the gamut: from single player games that pit you against the artificial intelligence of the computer, to Massively Multiplayer Online Games (MMOGs) that can immerse hundreds or even thousands of people in the game at the same time.

Single Player

Single player games may either be designed only for one player, or contain multiplayer options. Players match their wits against the computer. One-player games tend to have more involved story lines, and include many adventure, role-playing and strategy games. Single player elements also appear in sports and action games.

Multiplayer Games

Once you tire of competing with your computer, multiplayer games offer you the chance to compete with others online. All sorts of Internet games involve multiplayer formats—everything from action games like Quake III Arena (a big teen favorite) to tried and true amusements like Hearts, Scrabble, and Poker. Thousands regularly play against one another on sites like Yahoo!Games and Microsoft's Zone.com.

Massively Multiplayer Online Games (MMOG's)

A third category specific to the Internet are Massively Multiplayer Online Games (MMOGs). These games have no single player component, and are played entirely online. Players experience the game with hundreds or even thousands of other players at once.

The most popular MMOGs are role-playing games, where thousands of players can connect to a server, create characters, and interact with others in real-time, with a graphical representation of themselves to serve as a kind of "avatar." Most of these games create an entire fantasy world, through which players—in the guise of characters—explore the new world, attempt to learn new skills, gain experience, and amass hoards of gold and treasure. All the while they can carry on long conversations, cooperate with one another, or attack one another.

Some players, particularly teens, feel more comfortable interacting in this virtual world than in the "real" one. Teens, particularly those going through an awkward social stage, can find these worlds welcoming.

A few warnings about MMOGs: like Internet chat rooms, these games can include speech you don't want your child to "hear." Some players can overdose; my 16-year-old has several friends who spend more time in "Everquest" than they do in school. As Craig Wessel, author of *A Parent's Guide to Computer Games* notes, "If you generally limit the time your children spend before a computer or television, this might not be the best game for them to get started on."

Freeware, Shareware, Demos, and 'Mods'

Before we start playing, let's begin with some basic information about how to access games online.

Freeware and shareware rule at Shockwave.com.

Finding games online is simple, but it helps first to know what games you're after. While sites like Games (**www.games.com**) or Shockwave (**www.shockwave.com**) can quickly put you online with other players, for other games, you'll need to download software before jumping into the game. Game software (and most other software) available online can be divided into several types.

Freeware

Freeware is programming available at no cost to you. To access freeware, you simply need to download it. You need to remember, however, that much freeware is copyrighted, which means you can't use it or copy it into your own programming.

Shareware

Shareware is distributed free on a trial basis with the understanding that you may need or want to pay for it later. Some software developers offer a shareware version of programs with a built-in expiration date (after 30 days or 20 uses, for example, the user can no longer get access to the program). Shareware can also be offered with certain capabilities disabled as an enticement to buy the complete version of the program. Lots of great games—arcade, board and action, among others, can be found at CNET.com (**http://shareware.cnet.com**).

Postcardware

This no-charge software is freely shared with one caveat: users are required to send the software provider a postcard as a form of payment. The idea is to humanize the transaction, reminding the user that someone else shared something freely, and for the provider, to let him know that someone is actually using the creation.

Demos

A sample download of a commercial product that you can buy in a store, a demo is usually a "taste" of the real game, sometimes with additional characters and new sequences. Demo downloads can be found at a number of sites. One of our favorites is Happy Puppy (**www.happypuppy.com**), although parents should watch out for violence. A site devoted exclusively non-violent games on demos from Russia is YAV Games (**www.yavsort.com**).

Game Modifcations or "Mods"

Another hot source of online games are extensions or variations of familiar video games. These are add-on software to games designed and developed by people for sole release on the Net. Mod designers are often fans of a certain game, who might want to extend the life of a game.

Modification of the popular Half-Life, Counter-Strike is the most popular game played online.

While the content of "mods" generally ape that of the original game, designers have free reign, since the original designer has no hand in the mod. This might mean a rise in violent or graphic content. Because of this, you might want to check on what your child downloads before giving them the go-ahead.

A Few Words to the Wise

Games cost a lot to design. And they draw a lot of people onto the Net. Add these two elements together and you spell a big advertising opportunity, which means that game sites—and sometimes games themselves—are heavily larded with ads: banners, pop-ups, or even promotions worked into the games. If your kids are susceptible to these sorts of come-ons (clicking onto every flashing banner, for example), you might want to help them differentiate between what is flak and what is actually the game.

Along with ads, not all game portals that link to kids' games are targeted to kids. Casino gambling games or other pastimes that you might not find appropriate for your children might be listed right next to an innocent round of checkers.

The Challenge: Have Fun!

Interactive Playing

Noah and Sasha share an enthusiasm for Shockwaves' "Inklink"—a clever test of verbal and art skills that requires participants to illustrate a word or phrase. Then, three to eight participants compete to guess what your scribbling signifies. While your sketch appears onscreen, contestants' best guesses pop up in chat room format on either side of your masterpiece.

One nice element of this game is that even if you need all the help you can get when it comes to actual art, players tend to be supportive and innovative in their guesses. During a recent round, for example, we confronted a reasonably recognizable unicorn, a completely baffling piece of cardboard (Chocolate bar? Kite? Paper bag?), and a conceptually challenging "Fast"—illustrated by a two cars, one with a radar gun aimed out of the window.

Newbie's can gather together in one room, while more advanced players congregate in other areas, which helps if a) you are new to the game, or b) you're not new, but your drawing and guessing skills continue to require fine tuning. (If you get desperate, think of the contestant who spelled out "p-a-n," then drew a cake spiked with candles… Pancake? Get it??)

Quiz Games and Crosswords

Trivia games and quizzes of various complexities pop up all over the Web. Since Noah and I are partial to Harry Potter and baseball, we tend to concentrate on these areas, and, luckily for us, there are no dearth of questions, crosswords or puzzles to test our knowledge. But if wizards and homeruns aren't your stock in trade, don't worry. You can find Web sites that test everything from obscure Shakespeare quotes to what to do in a natural disaster. If you can know it, chances are pretty good that someone has devised a way to worm it from your brain.

Feeling up for a challenge, Noah and I headed for Quizland (**www.quizland.com**) a site packed with free trivia games. There, after skimming a batch of intriguing possibilities that ranged from trivia questions on soda pop to George Bush (and a Kids Quiz that we promised to return to later) we settled on a contest called "Think You're So Smart?"

After warning us that the questions were harder than they looked, we were offered the choice to take our questions with or without music. (Simple, repetitive music is supposed to improve mental function, or so say the quiz's authors. Think "Jeopardy" and make up your own mind.) On the supposition that we need all the help we can get, we took the music.

Questions are weighed by how many contestants have guessed wrong in the past. For example, if 48% of 215,770 visitors got the question wrong, it's worth 48 points. (That particular question had to do with whether or not poinsettias were poisonous to humans and let's just say that now that Noah and I have contributed to the tally, the number of erroneous visitors has risen to 215,771.)

After my poinsettia fallacy, Noah took the driver's seat. (Did Noah remember Boggle?) Questions were pretty much multiple choice or true/false and though they could be tricky (What was the definition of Mafia?) they weren't exactly Nobel-prize level (How many cities are named after U.S. Presidents?).

Anyway, not to brag, but in that single round, working more or less together, we raked in 374 points, which put us among the Top Scorers. Noah was all for throwing a victory party, but remembering our miserable Boggle experience, I decided to treat our new status with a bit more humility. We settled on cookies and milk.

Quizland contains some games unsuitable for kids, so it's best to stay by your child's side. Also, there are well-identified ads on the site that can be tempting for little fingers.

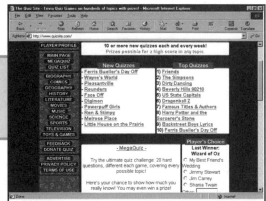

Popular culture quizzes challenge players on www.quizsite.com.

Fantasy Baseball for Kids

Fantasy baseball, where you choose and run an entire team for the season, is a great way to interact online, but most teams cover long stretches of time and involve complex organizing skills, good for adults and teens, but a little complicated for those at Little League levels. To answer this problem while giving kids the excitement of fantasy sports, "Sports Illustrated for Kids" has put together a nice site called Bat-O-Matic (**www.sikids.com/fantasy/baseball**) where kids can run their own team under the guiding eyes of the "Commish."

After registering on to the site, budding team managers receive $4,500,000 (not for real, it's a game) to lure 9 draft prospects to their team. This requires some math and advanced planning. As the rules note, don't go drafting Mark McGwire unless you plan to have that kid who keeps smashing tennis balls into your parents' back window field third. For those whose appetite for the big names proves bigger than their budgets, if you mess up (Mark is a pretty good home-run hitter...), the "Commish" will step in to reject your lineup, and it's back to scouting again.

Rankings are based on real games, and there are 12 separate seasons to run your team, with points awarded at the close of each season. It's a nice way to interact with the All-American past time, and your child.

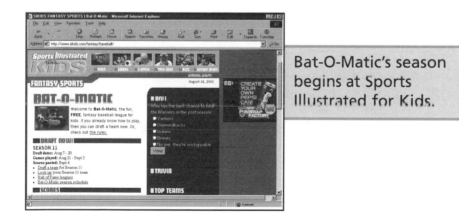

Bat-O-Matic's season begins at Sports Illustrated for Kids.

Projects: A Deeper Look at Games

Whether or not you think kids can get "addicted" to games (I happen to think kids can get obsessed by almost anything), teaching your kids to step back and think about the games they play can pay off in big ways in developing their analytic skills. The following projects can help kids take a deeper look at the games people play.

→ **What Makes a Game Good?** As online games become more interactive with other computer software, talk to your kids about what draws and keeps them playing some interactive games and not others. What games do they like and why? What makes a game worth returning to? Are there similarities between games and books they enjoy? For example, does a good game—much like a good book—tell a story that makes you want to find out how it ends? One of the draws of Super Mario Bros., a popular video game on the Super Nintendo console, was to finally rescue that princess. (I know one young child who burst into tears when the quest was finally successful.)

→ **Geoff Howland**, an articulate and thoughtful game designer and owner of Lupine Games, has written an interesting article on what makes interactive games "addictive." Factors he cites include the narrative need to see the game end, a desire to 'master' the game, a competitive drive to beat high scorers, and the interest in exploring and perhaps finding new unknown or hidden game levels or locations. As a game designer, he brings interesting insights that can help your kids understand what makes a game so involving, something you want to return to again and again.

→ **Do your kids agree?** Can they add any factors? Do they have ideas about how to improve the design of a game they play to make it more involving?

→ **Learn how to play an old game using new technology.** Have a nine-year-old who wants to learn Parcheesi, Othello, or Go? Download rules and apply them to the game. Play the game online, then on a board. How does the experience change? How does it stay the same? Which is more involving?

→ **Pick a topic to play.** What's your kids' passion? Is she a tennis freak (**www.tennislovers.com/index2.htm?games/onlinegames.htm**) or a budding chess expert (**http://games.yahoo.com**)? Does he adore Harry Potter or that Lemony Snicket trio Baudelaire? Go online to find games around your favorite topic, and then challenge your child to an hour of online games in their favorite flavor. Mix them up with puzzles, slides, quizzes, and visual adventure games.

→ **Make your own game 1.** Taking a look at the elements that make up a game and then going online to manipulate elements or create their own can help kids "deconstruct" games. At the Clever Media site (**http://clevermedia.com**), kids can put together basic elements of a game, and then execute it. Although it's kind of limited as to options, it can start a discussion about games and the sorts of actions that make games exciting. Similar discussion provoking sites include: Build-A-Monster (**www.goobo.com/monster**), Wacky Web Tales (**www.eduplace.com/tales**) where kids can write their own stories and submit them in the ever-popular "Mad-Lib" format, and for small kids, the I Spy site at Scholastic(**www.scholastic.com/ispy/make/index.htm**)where kids can submit a riddle and/or picture to help with the game.

For small fry, check out build a monster on www.goobo.com.

→ **Make your own game 2.** Remember those old text adventure games?
"You are in a room. You see a box, a window, and an exit to the west."
Then you type a command: Open the box.
"Music comes out of the box and a ballerina twirls"
Throw box out window.
"You are in a room. You see a broken window, and an exit to the west."
These days, such games are called Interactive Fiction. You can download editors to build and programs to run your creation from the interactive fiction/adventure games site at **http://interactfiction.about.com**.

Machines & Games

Many games online are played against the computer, but some games are more heavily focused on competent artificial intelligence than others. If you and your child want to find out more on how this works, you might want to explore The Game AI Site, where you can find links to:

MindPixel:...**www.mindpixel.com/**

This isn't exactly a "game," but it's a chance to be part of an amazing data gathering project that will eventually teach GAC (pronounced Jack) what it is to be human—perhaps the trickiest game of all. How? By offering a mindpixel—a question that can be answered yes or no. i.e. All water is wet, 2+2=5—then going on to respond to twenty other mindpixels offered by others. This information, which will eventually number one billion Mindpixels, will then be used to train neural Net-based systems to mimic a human being when presented with Mindpixels.

Robocup: .... **www.robocup.org/**

By the year 2050, robocup enthusiasts plan to develop a team of fully autonomous humanoid robots that can compete against (and defeat) the human world soccer champions. Track their progress and process.

Twenty Questions:.. **www.oozinggoo.com/20q/**

A game that learns from its mistakes, and applies its' new knowledge towards the next player.

Learning Online

Chapter 7

Class Rooms, Homeschooling, and Distance Learning Online

Make no mistake about it. The buzzword in education—from kindergarten classes to post graduate seminars—is technology. How can technology best be employed to prepare kids for the world changed by—you guessed it—technology? What technological skills will our kids need to be successful? How will technology change the role of the teacher in the classroom? Will working the Web make kids smarter—or lazier? How might technology affect student-teacher relationships? What are the best ways for teachers to evaluate the impact of technology on learning, social skills, and creativity?

In short: now that most American classrooms are wired to the Internet, what's next?

Some school districts across the country have already enthusiastically joined Internet projects such as the National Science Foundation or National Humanities Programs. These projects revolutionize ways to learn and teach: going on "Web-quests" to Antarctica or whaling in Massachusetts, coordinating projects with nursing home residents, or assembling a world-wide cookbook. Other schools, as yet unsure how new technologies fit into their existing programs, have proceeded with greater caution.

Advanced Placement Courses

Serc	www.serc.org
StarNet	www.starnet.org
Oklahoma State University	http://extension.okstate.edu/k12.htm
Mt. Plains Distance Learning Partnership-STARS	http://stars-cwc.cwc.cc.wy.us
Class.com	www.class.com
The Florida High School	www.fhs.net
Kentucky Virtual High School	www.kvhs.org

Online and Correspondence K-12 Courses

Distance Learning Exchange	www.dle.state.pa.us
Cyberschool	http://cyberschool.4j.lane.edu
Jefferson County Public School District	www.jeffco.k12.co.us
Laurel Springs	www.laurelsprings.com
The University of Florida Division of Continuing Education	www.doce.ufl.edu
Internet Academy	www.iaacademy.org

"Technology means so many different things to different people," says Kyle Peck, Ph.D, Professor of Education at Penn State University. "But the use of technologies shouldn't be 'about' the technologies—it should be about improving student learning."

To Peck, the new "technologically rich" education environment is not only about gathering information, but about learning how to navigate, critically judge, and build something important using the information. To accomplish this, kids need to work in more concrete fashion and in collaboration with other students, teachers and outside experts, and communities online.

This combination will lead to radical changes not only in what and how kids learn, but working with this new technology, there'll develop a new "tenacity in kids to discover by doing."

How Do Teachers Use the Internet?

A survey conducted in the spring of 1999 by the National Center for Educational Statistics found that 99 percent of full-time regular public school teachers reported they had access to computers or the Internet somewhere in their schools. Of these teachers:

→ Thirty-nine percent used computers or the Internet to create instructional materials. Less than 10 percent reported using computers or the Internet to access model lesson plans or to access research.

→ Newer teachers were more likely to use computers or the Internet in their teaching.

→ Poverty levels influenced the use of the Internet. Schools with a poverty level below 11 percent were more likely to use computers or the Internet for creating instructional materials (52 percent), while teachers with a school poverty level of 71 percent or more did so only 32 percent of the time.

→ Of the sixty-six percent of public school teachers who used computers during class time, about a third (30 percent) reported assigning research using the Internet to a moderate or large extent. The balance used computer time for applications like word processing or spread sheets.

→ Elementary teachers were more likely than secondary school teachers to use computers for practice drills and to have kids use computers or the Internet to solve problems. Secondary teachers were more likely to assign research using the Internet (41 to 25 percent). (Source, "Teachers Use of Computers and the Internet in Public Schools'" **www.nces.ed.gov/pub-search/pubsinfo.asp?pubid=2000090.**)

The Connected Classroom

Technology in the classroom provides tools for learning. New technologies, like the Internet, can help kids and teachers create better learning environments and stretch the possibilities of 'old,' but still important, technologies like books and blackboards.

"Kids can use scissors," says Catherine Schifter, associate professor in the Department of Curriculum, Instruction & Technology in Education at Temple University in Philadelphia, PA. "But they don't want to use scissors all day long. The same is true of classroom technology. It's part of the learning experience—not all of it."

"The Web isn't a substitute for books," says Schifter. "There are still things which you can find in a library—rare documents, rare books—that can't be accessed online. There is the sensual experience of books that's also important for kids. But the Internet is one tool of many that can help learning."

To Schifter, one of the best uses of the Net will be in giving students more options in the classroom. "Kids will have more ways to learn. And teachers will have more ways to teach. All of which means a change in the culture of the 'one-size-fits-all' classroom."

One profound shift, says Peck, will be the role of the teacher. Rather than a teacher who stands before a classroom imparting knowledge, Peck envisions the teacher of the near future as a kind of "travel agent," someone who helps kids get where they need to go.

"Teachers will collaborate with kids who have technology skills," he says. This collaboration will not only encourage kids to share what they know, upping their independence and self-esteem, but also aid in increasing teacher tech skills.

Most educators agree that simply sitting a child or teenager in front of a computer doesn't guarantee better learning. Mindlessly clicking around the Net can be a deadening, rather than a learning experience. Kids who spend more time picking cool fonts for a Web-based report, rather than thinking through ideas, writing, or planning the report have benefited little from the experience. For this reason, Peck strongly recommends that kids have a clear goal when they're working with technology, so they have little inclination to stray.

"Kids with goals become confident in their abilities to figure out what needs to be done and to do it," he says.

Peck sees many changes over the next ten years in the American classroom. "It will be more important for kids to know how to access and use knowledge rather than memorizing facts."

How can technology change classrooms in the future?

→ **Connect learning with real life.** Rather than learning text from a book or solving 'made up' problems, kids will spend more time working and thinking about real world problems in their communities and beyond. This may mean working with scientists, gathering data on their environment. One example is the GLOBE project (**www.globe.gov/fsl/welcome.html**). Here, students from around the world learn to take scientifically valid measurements of their regional atmosphere, hydrology, and soil and land cover for use by scientists. Kids can create maps and graphics using interactive resources at the site, as well as collaborate with scientists and other study participants. Having the chance to deal with experts online offers kids a unique opportunity not only to understand how scientists work, but to communicate and collaborate with people on the cutting edge of research. In much the same way, technologies let students instantly access real world data, news, and problems-scenarios.

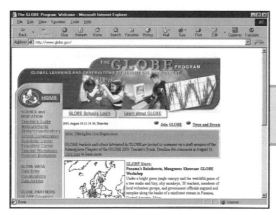

The GLOBE environmental classroom home page.

→ **Allow teachers to tailor teaching styles to each student's needs and learning styles.** Technology can help kids move at their own pace. Rather than present content to kids at the same pace, teachers can create learning goals, and then send kids to specific materials that guide them through the information. One nice example is the Urban Programs Resource Network from the University of Illinois extension program (**www.urbanext.uiuc.edu/kids/index.html**). In the "My First Garden" section, 4th grade students learn basic plant facts, including instruction on planting both at home and at school.

→ **Shift the role of the teacher**. Technology frees teachers from the need to deliver information to students while making it easier to give frequent feedback to kids on their work. "Kids will go to teachers to draw on their knowledge and experience about topics, to ask questions when they get stuck, to bounce off ideas, and get their feedback." In this model, teachers can go online to communicate with kids and their parents about their progress.

→ **Permit greater collaboration with teachers, peers, and experts.** Collaborative projects involving teachers, students, and experts, help students to understand complicated systems and concepts. WhaleNet (**http://whale.wheelock.edu**) has established Internet communication between researchers and students from around the world so that they can share and use research data, collaborative learning, and personal field experiences to enhance their education and interest in science. WhaleNet provides a system where students, teachers, and researchers collect and then compile their data on the WhaleNet server. The data is then shared, via WhaleNet, with schools for interdisciplinary curricular activities and student research in their respective classrooms world-wide.

Run with the Whales at Whale Net.

→ **Connect kids with other students and experts from different locations.** "What works in education, regardless of the medium of communication, are intelligent, caring adults spending lots of quality contact time with children in a close one-on-one setting," says Barry Kort, a founding Director of MicroMuse, and the first Multi-User Simulation Environment (MUSE) site fully dedicated to educational purposes.

→ **Classrooms have set up projects** with experts a few miles or a few thousand miles away.

→ **Other student conversations take place** as online project activities for the class. They can be part of structured online learning environments or programs, or may be part of a class activity. Students can interact on project topics under the guidance of a teacher with online experts and other teachers or students. One program, e-Pals (**www.epals.com**) gives students a chance to discuss particular topics of universal interest. Past subjects of discussions included conversations on "the digital divide" between rich, and poor countries when it comes to technology, and where, under the guidance of teachers, global participants took turns writing a single mythic story.

→ **Teach students to use electronic portfolios** and reflective journals to examine their learning goals and thinking processes. Online portfolios reflecting a student's progress provide a way to review work and for kids to express in their own ways what they've learned about their research and accumulated learning. See **www.clccharter.org** for some great examples of sites composed by students at CLC Charter School in State College, PA.

→ **Use online simulations** to teach students the scientific process of generating and testing hypotheses for science classes. Although it will be closing in January 2002, a great example of how this works is the Biological Timing Online Science Experiment designed for K-4 and Middle School students (**www.cbt.virginia.edu/Olh**). Funded by the National Science Foundation (NSF), the project involved four universities and one research institute who worked to unearth the mysteries of biological clocks. Using a "Hamster Cam" kids were taught scientific techniques of observational animal research. Committed to bringing the "joy of discovery" to pre-college aged kids, the project is designed so that kids are not only observers, but actual participants in the experiments. Noted scientists plan to remain in regular communication as mentors, with the hope that kids interested in science will continue to stay in touch.

→ **Employ Educational MOOs.** MOOs (Multiuser Object-Oriented environments) give students a chance to build and interact in a shared virtual space. At the Romantic High School Web site, an online network of teachers and students dedicated to the study of the humanities, you can enter a MOO environment and explore ideas about 19th century lit with classes around the world. Students in a MOO can chat with one another, visit assigned Web sites, and hand in projects. (Join the MOO as a guest at **www.rc.umd.edu/rchs/rchsmoo.html**).

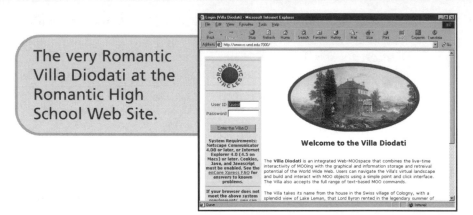

The very Romantic Villa Diodati at the Romantic High School Web Site.

While some schools have fully adopted and adapted their curriculum to take advantage of newly available technologies and the Internet, others have voyaged more cautiously into this new frontier. Aside from the cost of new technologies, several other factors explain these differences in approach.

Serious and thoughtful arguments between educational thinkers about how best to employ technology in the classroom paper the Web. In addition, like many parents not bred on these new technologies, many teachers have yet to feel comfortable with the Internet. In a survey conducted in the spring of 1999 by the National Center for Educational Statistics, ten percent of teachers questioned said they were "very well prepared" to use the Internet to teach, while less than a quarter (23 percent) said they were "well prepared" to add Internet to their class-rooms. This group of teachers was also more likely to assign projects involving corresponding with authors, experts, or students from other schools. (See box: "How Do Teachers Use the Internet?")

While state governments, school boards, and teachers' colleges rush to fill the gap in technology skills for new and experienced teachers, other issues continue to be addressed when it comes to computers and the public school classrooms of America.

→ **Should all learning be fun?** Critics object to the idea that by sitting down and clicking onto a computer, students are automatically learning. Learning, they insist, is and should be hard work. Computers, say these critics, with their emphasis on immediate gratification, visual effects, and 'edutainment' fragment attention spans and delay actual learning as kids sift through extraneous stuff.

→ **How can we address the Digital Divide?** The gap between those people and communities with access to information technology and those without it has been labeled the Digital Divide. Yet there are many smaller divides, characterized by community, ethnic or economic factors, age groups, and abilities to access and utilize digital technologies. *The Condition of Education 2000*, released by the National Center for Educational Statistics in 2001, shows that in 1998, 78 percent of students in grades 1-12 used the Internet in school. However, white students in those grades were more likely than Black or Hispanic students to have Internet access at school (83 percent vs. 70 and 71, respectively). Students from higher income bracket families were also more likely than low to middle class students to use the Internet while at school (86 percent vs. 68 and 78 percent, respectively.)

According to *Falling Through the Net: Towards Digital Inclusion*, published in 2000 by the National Telecommunications and Information Association, groups that had traditionally been digital "have nots" have made dramatic gains since 1994. Yet despite these gains, large gaps still remain for Black and Hispanic households when it comes to being connected at home. Schools, libraries, and other public service access points continue to serve groups that do not have access at home. (For more information on the digital divide and what can be done about it, see **www.digitaldivide.gov**)

The George Lucas Educational Foundation (GLEF) creates media that tries to combat the digital divide by promoting an understanding of learning in which children are challenged and engaged, have access to interactive technologies, and are supported by inspired teachers and involved parents and communities. (see **http://glcf.org**).

→ **What about censorship?** Like public libraries, public schools have had to address the issue of filtering information over the Web. Situations where blocking such words as "breast" prevent inappropriate graphic material but also information about breast cancer research have raised free speech issues, particularly in high schools. In addition to filtering software, many schools have "acceptable use" policies, which often prohibit posting messages on chat rooms, message boards, or mailing lists. "E-rate" legislation has also forced public schools that receive federal funds to shield minors from "objectionable materials." Several sites, including the Center for Technology and Democracy, address these free speech issues (see **www.ctd.org**).

The Internet and Homeschooling

When it comes to homeschooling, diversity is the rule. Just as parents differ in why they choose to homeschool their children, from religious to academic reasons, so does how they tailor the homeschooling experience. Approaches to homeschooling range from "unschooling"—where parents tailor learning to a child's interests, to a traditional approach, where kids follow the textbook and test approach followed by many schools.

Because of these differences, individual homeschooling parents use the Internet in many different ways. Some restrict their use to research, while others encourage their kids to join science projects, communicate with experts, or even take distance learning courses to supplement their homeschool experience.

Among the benefits for homeschoolers online:

➜ **Curriculum.** Most requirements of state curriculum can be found on the Internet. Cyber schools also provide classes and model curriculum online. Kids can sign up with virtual schools that offer curriculum, courses, and contacts with other home-schooled kids.

➜ **Social connections.** One criticism of homeschooling is that it robs kids of the chance to communicate and interact with classmates. Using e-mail, listservs, IRC chat, MOOs, bulletin boards, and IM, kids can interact in new ways that cater to their interests. (For listservs in the classroom, check out the Distance Learning Resources Network at **www.dlrn.org/**.)

➜ **Calendars.** To help kids keep track of their assignments, many homeschool parents set up a password protected online calendar so kids can log in anytime to see what's expected of them.

➜ **Virtual field trips.** Travel from the bottom of the ocean to outer space becomes possible online.

Linking Learners

Kidlink (**www.kidlink.org**) provides listservs for K-12 students. A non-profit, grassroots group, KIDLINK connects kids globally. Most of the networking takes place in listservs, but they also sponsor Web-based dialogues, video conferencing, and real-time IRC chat. There are many KID forum discussion group conferences.

KIDCAFE-TOPICS mailing lists are for open dialogue including both individual exchanges (keypals) and group discussions or inquiries on topics introduced by the kids. The number of Kidcafes and rules for participation differ by language area. KIDFORUM mailing lists are open for one discussion at a time, for about two months per topic. Adult moderators work with participating students and their instructors.

When it comes to the Internet, homeschooling parents note that it is a tool, not a solution. Marsha Ransom, author of *The Idiot's Guide to Homeschooling*, finds the Internet most effective in downloading preplanned units of study, or to research answers for specific research questions.

Laura Fokkena, whose seven-year-old home-schooled daughter Rayaka uses the Internet to track daily and monthly assignments, communicate with special interest groups, and to travel to virtual archeological digs, notes that many of the "education" sites that claim to be educational are nothing more than interactive advertisements of a particular product.

"The last message I want my daughter to get is the notion that she's worthless unless she's wearing the right pair of jeans. I'm no fan of porn, but it's relatively easy to avoid. Advertising, on the other hand, is ubiquitous, aimed at children and absolutely relentless. It's easy to say that people of my generation lived through commercials and it didn't do me any harm. Advertisers spend 20 times more on marketing to kids than they did 10 years ago. We need to invest much more in time and energy in media literacy before letting kids loose into this sort of environment." She also finds that while connecting with kids who share her daughter's interests is great, hanging out on the Britney Spears site is another matter, entirely.

More on Homeschooling from Parent's Guide Press

Homeschooling families have a lot to gain from the Internet. Great lesson plans are easily found, as are virtual field trips, and scads of opportunities for, not to mention fun, friends and interactive games when it's time to take a break from schoolwork. Trouble only comes along when the Net turns into something that a family either completely avoids or completely depends on. Each perspective is skewed and will create its own set of problems.

The family that avoids computers and/or the Internet is denying their children access to skills and information they will most likely need for the rest of their lives. Whether people like the idea or not, today's culture is definitely computer oriented and there are very few jobs or directions in life a person can take that won't include the need for some element of computer savvy. Learning how to operate a computer, log on to the Net and use its resources will not only enhance a child's education, but also make him/her more employable. For those parents who are reluctant to bring the Internet into their children's lives, here are some suggestions:

* Learn about how to access the Internet yourself and how it can help.
* Limit the amount of time your kids spend on the Internet.
* Only allow access to the Internet if you are sitting with your kids.
* Don't purchase a computer for your home and instead use those found your local library or a friend's home.

—Tamra Orr

Distance Learning

Virtual schools and online classes fill the Internet, offered by everyone from MIT to fly-by-night commercial outfits. While the opening of educational opportunities is thrilling, you need to examine programs with care to see how well they're constructed and whether they fit your child's individual needs.

Teachers also need to look at courses to see how well they can be taught using computer technologies. "The teacher-student relationship online is different than that in a classroom," acknowledges Stephen J. Jones, Ph.D, a communication professor at University of Illinois at Chicago. "Courses often need to be redesigned to take that into consideration. Teachers need to find new ways of evaluating students understanding, since they can't 'see' whether they truly do comprehend material."

How do you evaluate courses online? The Distance Learning Resource Network, a government organization, suggests looking at the following areas:

→ **Examine the qualifications of the sponsoring organization.** While no set accreditation process exists for distance learning courses, many programs are backed by reliable colleges or virtual schools.

→ **Accountability and preparedness of teachers.** How will work be assigned, gathered, or assessed? Whether work is accepted in hardcopy or electronic format, the DLRN suggests that essays or projects evaluate progress better than multiple-choice formats. This not only aids in familiarizing instructors with student's work, but it can help a teacher better evaluate a student's understanding of concepts and to pinpoint problems.

→ **Accreditation.** Will courses be recognized by colleges? High school students—particularly those who have a specific university in mind—should check this before they enroll.

→ **Structure.** Check to see if the course starts and ends at a certain date or if the student will have a flexible amount of time to finish the course at her own pace.

→ **Administration.** How is the course delivered? Weekly, daily, monthly?

→ **Teacher to student ratios.** Experts suggest that the ratio of students should be no more than 25 to 1 and no less than 8 to 1.

Distance learning can also be a more private affair. University professors, computer experts, or art historians (to name a few) may agree to take on a private pupil or two via the Net.

Research and the Web

By the time kids reach middle school, chances are good that most of their information will come from the Web. For this reason, kids need to know how to critically evaluate information and how to judge what information fits their needs.

Towards Media Literacy

To become media literate, kids need to practice evaluating online material. Among questions they might consider:

→ Does the site cover the topic comprehensively and accurately?

→ Are the links well-chosen? Are they up-to-date?

→ How current is the information on the site? When was the site last revised?

→ Can you get better information from another source?

→ Who is responsible for the site? What are their credentials? Have they cited their sources? What is the domain: .edu, .gov or .com?

→ Can you find a bias on the site?

Smart Sites

The Kids on the Web **www.zen.org/~brendan/kids.html**
A wonderful collection of links to kids' Web pages, projects, and information for adults about life and kids online.

Franklin Institute Hot Site **http://sln.fi.edu/tfi/hotlists/interactive.html**

Ology Site
(American Museum of National History)
http://ology.amnh.org/index.html

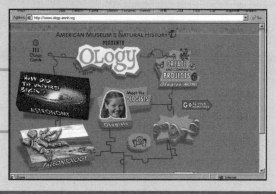

What's fun about science?
Find out at the 'Ology' site.

Projects: Education

→ **Compare and contrast.** Along with your child, look up a subject on a dot-org site and then a dot-com site. How does the information differ? How is it alike? Check the research you found online against a textbook or a library source. Is it accurate? Is it fair?

→ **Quiz the experts.** Find a university site and e-mail a question to an expert in a field that interests you.

→ **Create a puzzle online.** Go to **www.puzzlemaker.com** and, together with your son or daughter, try to make a puzzle of every state capitol. Or every flower name you can think of. Or, how about every sugary cereal you can dream up?

→ **Stay in touch** with your kids' homework on a teacher page or by e-mail.

→ **Create an online calendar** of your child's homework assignments and long-term goals. (Be sure to include treat and game nights.)

→ **For teachers (or parents) looking for inspiration,** Melissa Matusevich's Web site on projects she designed for Virginia schools during the 1990s is a good jumping off point (**http://pixel.cs.vt.edu/melissa/projects.html**). Listed are a number of ways to involve the larger community with kids' learning.

Evaluating Information

A number of sites help evaluate online materials. Among them:

Bookmark Tutorial—Evaluating Resources ....**www.infopeople.org/bkmk/select.html**

Evaluating Internet Resources..................**http://library.albany.edu/internet/evaluate.html**

Kathy Schrock's Guide
for Educators—
Critical Evaluation Surveys..................**http://school.discovery.com/schrockguide/eval.html**

Teens
Online

Chapter 8

Teens Online

For your consideration: a portrait of Sasha, my computer competent sixteen-year-old.

On almost any night of the school year, if you open Sasha's bedroom door past nine-thirty or so, you'll find my oldest seated at his computer (composed of parts that he and his Dad pieced together from components purchased at various computer shows), his fingers pacing the keyboard, gaze crossing the constantly flickering screen. Around him waft the cool tones of Miles Davis notes rising from an MP3 Sash downloaded and burned onto a CD. Intent, he scans the second draft of a term paper for his tenth grade American history class: Horace Mann, an early education reformer. Between bursts of word processing, he flips to the Web to read primary sources for the paper, and then back to his e-mail, an ongoing game of *The Age of Empires*, all the while fielding beeps from his IM buddies.

You might think that Sasha is unfocused, but let me add that he's a straight A student. If anything, he has the ability—shared by many of his digital generation—to divide and fix on many, many things at once. His ability to navigate his way through so many screens of information is called multi-tasking, and his friends, boys and girls alike, share this dexterity. These kids, generation x and y, were born to the Net.

Marketers, as will be discussed later in the book, have grabbed onto this transformed consciousness. Or, as a report on *Wired Teens* from Forrester, Inc., a research firm that specializes in Internet issues, notes: "While adults adopt the Net and 16- to 22- year-olds internalize it, these kids have the Internet burned into their brains."

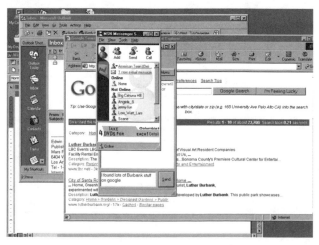

But what's interesting—and encouraging—is that far from falling for marketing ploys or spending their time pursuing merchandise on retail sites, a large number of teens have taken the Net as their own, bending and using it to fit their own needs. For many, including my son Sash, learning the Net has made them more curious about programming computers, what lies under the interface, and they've spent time literally taking computers apart, teaching themselves C++, Java, and other languages that aren't offered in school. It's opened new ways to research for school—Sash has read everything from Gwendolyn Brooks to the transcript of the Chicago Eight trial online. The Net has revealed new worlds of interests as kids download and listen to the history of the blues, watch streaming video cooking shows, and play complicated multiplayer games online. Information arrives in many distinctive packets from CNN to Matt Drudge.

For other teens, the Net has become a venue for self-revelation and discovery, as kids have created their own magazines, e-zines, Web pages, and Web logs (or 'Blogs') that often include poetry, art, wicked cartoons, and—in the spirit of every teen who ever lived—endless navel gazing at the hell that can be growing into your teenage skin. The Web has given marginalized groups—gay teens, ethnic teens, shy teens, female teens, ways to express themselves and meet others who can share their stories. The Web has also spawned a way for kids to take power in a way that they might not in their real lives: kids protest against global corporate exploitation, kids work to circumvent censorship in their schools.

Yet what about the dangers online? Don't teens worry about their safety?

Based on several studies, these Net savvy teens not only use the Internet in their own ways, but know how to protect themselves. As Amanda Lenhart, the principal author of the Pew study, *Teenage Life Online: The rise of the instant-message generation and the Internet's impact on friendships and family relationships* notes, "Kids have mastered the technology and are confident that they can handle what the Net throws at them."

Instant Messaging

"The Internet is the telephone, television, game console, and radio wrapped up in one for teenagers," says Lee Rainie, Director of the Pew Internet & American Life Project. "Teens use online tools to chat with their friends, kill boredom, see the wider world and follow the latest trends. Many enjoy doing all those things at the same time online."

Instant Messaging, popularly known as IM or IMing, occupies a top spot in teen time online, according to the Pew Internet Study on Teenage Life Online. Three-quarters of the 754 teens between age 12 and 17 surveyed for the study use instant messaging, compared to less than half of their parents (44 percent).

My on-site teen fits comfortably into this statistic: most nights he simply leaves his AOL Instant Messenger (AIM) on all of the time he's online, in case he gets a buddy beep.

Basically, IM is like a text-based telephone: users carry on a back and forth conversation with one or (this is where it gets fun) two or three or four or more buddies at the same time (multi-tasking again). The system lets you identify if a pal is online, and if they are, you can 'message' them immediately.

AOL first popularized IM. But even if you don't subscribe to AOL, you can get connected by downloading software from the AOL site for free. Other versions of instant chat, all available online for free, include Yahoo! IM, ICQ ("I seek you"), and, at jabber.com, several 'free software' Instant Messengers that try to link all the popular IMs into a single network (much to the dismay of the AOLs, Yahoo!s and ICQs of the Net). Many include programs that permit real-time audio and video as well as text communications.

For IM to work, users have to be online at the same time, and the recipient has to be willing to accept instant messages. (You can set your software to reject messages.) If you try to IM someone not online, or who doesn't want to get your messages, you won't get through. But if your recipient is open to receive IMs, it alerts the recipient with a beep, a window that indicates the arrival of an IM, or a window that contains the incoming message.

Armed with this basic information, I sit down to have a chat online. Sash starts me off slowly, downloading the AIM software, and then putting himself on as the first buddy on my list. His own list has about sixty or so friends from all parts of his life: school, after-school activities, Sunday school, camp, etc.

Once we're connected, I take advantage of my first IM chat to question Sash about his IM use. He figures he spends about two hours a night using IM, which he judges is pretty typical for his friends. He also says that he's had some really good personal conversations on IM, but mainly in the one-on-one format. "It's easy to miss clues that you might find on the phone or in person. You lose sarcasm," he says, "and it's hard to be funny. Sometimes you're trying to be funny and the other person doesn't get it, so it can create misunderstandings."

On the other hand, Sash is awed by the lingo that has grown up on IM. "It's like a special language," he says, "because everything has to be communicated fast, like 'j/k' for just kidding." Kids also attach personal icons to identify themselves like musical notes or little cartoon figures, another quick identity marker.

Sash says that most of his buddies keep the IM on all the time they're online, just in case a conversation pops up. And most nights, he spends between one to two hours online. The Pew Internet study finds that his usage pattern is pretty near the norm. According to their findings, "close to half of young instant messengers say they spend between half and a full hour on instant messaging each time they do IM, and another 21 percent say they spend more than an hour on a typical session."

A Brief History of Napster

In 1999, nineteen-year-old Shawn Fanning created the free music swapping service, Napster. Napster permits users to trade music in an MP3 format with others online at the same time or to download music from the Napster site.

How does Napster work? To get music, you type in the name of an artist or song, then download the music from another person's hard drive. Users need to check the Napster directory frequently since what's available depends on who's online at the time.

Although Napster quickly became wildly popular (particularly among college students, whose stored collections of MP3s swamped many a college computer system), its fortunes turned downward in the face of challenges by various musicians and the Recording Industry Association of America, who accused Napster of 'music piracy.' Napster is expected to resurface, with a new subscription based, copyright friendly service.

About half the teens in the Pew Survey say being online strengthens friendships, although many realize it might not be the best way to develop deeper relationships or to meet new people. Like Sash, many teens in the survey feel that the Internet lets them be themselves and talk about issues that they might not otherwise deal with face-to-face.

Socially, the Internet also seems to help with romantic quandaries. A quarter of all boys say they've asked girls out on IM, and 13 percent of both sexes say they've used IM to break up. One commented, "Sometimes it is easier to say what is in your heart online. You can type the words and hit send instead of freezing up in person."

This brings up an interesting point about IM: despite the technological interface, it can be easier to have personal conversations or even to share personal revelations online. Released from face-to-face contact, shy teens may become bold. In this context, teens using IM, e-mail, and creating their own Web pages are part of what Sherry Turkel, Ph.D, a Massachusetts Technology researcher and author of "Life on the Screen: Identity in the Age of Internet," calls the "identity technology." Basically, using the new technology, people can try out new identities and explore their own identities online.

Why do kids (and some adults) feel 'safer' about exposing emotions online? Jon Suler, Ph.D, a psychology professor at Rider College in New Jersey who has examined this phenomenon, says that it's the very lack of face-to-face cues that make people feel safer. "You don't have to worry about how you look or how other people look when you reveal your emotions or something personal about yourself. The time delay in e-mail, and even in IM or chat, gives people more opportunity to compose their messages and hence, a greater feeling of control over the situation."

Overall, Suler sees this as another way kids get to experiment with their identities—just as they experiment with dress, hobbies, music, and social activities. Done in that spirit, experimenting with identities online may be part of that developmental process.

Music

Three or so years ago, Sasha tells me that he and his pal Ben downloaded Winamp (**www.winamp.com/**), a software application that permits you to play music in the MP3 format. But to their dismay, the two pre-teens found that they couldn't do a thing with it. Despite a frantic search, there were no name bands to download; no sounds that sounded good over their speakers. The few MP3s they did locate were of poor quality and by unknown artists.

Then a third friend mentioned the magic word: Napster.

"It was unbelievable," says Sash wistfully. "It was so good. There was a great selection, so easy. All we had to do was type in a song and the name of the artist."

Ah, Napster. In case you've been sleeping beneath a rock—which I doubt if you have kids—you know a little about Napster's legal problems. Although die-hard fans continue to insist that the music swapping service will rise from the legal restrictions placed on it at the insistence the music industry, at the moment of this writing, the original version of the free peer-to-peer music service is pretty much down and out.

Yet, all is not lost. Sash and his pals have turned to other services, like Audiogalaxy, Gnutella, Aimster, Toadnode.com, Morpheus Epitonic, Imesh, and others to take Napster's place. Known as 'peer-to-peer' technologies, these sites permit file-swapping of music via a decentralized system that is hard to control or trace. Because of this, they aren't quite as convenient to use as Napster, since there is no central index. They are also much less likely to be shut down by the music industry and the courts.

Removing my reporter's hat and retrieving my parental one, I ask Sash how legal these services are. He shrugs. But a little research reveals that Recording Industry Association of America (RIAA) is monitoring these new copycat services, and has sent out dozens of legal notices to Internet Service Providers (ISPs) providing connections for 'Open Napster' servers, which run the Napster-like software but are not associated with the company.

While the world waits to see what's going to become of Napster-like services and Napster itself, my resident expert notes that there are other music alternatives online, including jukebox like sites, called Music Match or Real Juke Box.

"Basically, these services make you a radio station to fit your picks," says Sash. "Say I plug in the Beatles and Miles Davis. Not only will they play those artists, but other artists who have similar sensibilities, plus give you information about the musicians, reviews of their work, and a place to buy the CD." Many of these use "streaming sound," sound that is played as it arrives. (As opposed to music that won't play until an entire file is downloaded, streaming sound can't easily be copied and re-distributed.)

One such service that has recently received very good reviews is MSN music, which has been billed as the 'anti-Napster.' MSN music lets you search for music using a browser and presents your picks in real time streaming music. You can add songs, artists, albums, or radio stations to your favorite's lists, but unlike Napster, you can't download songs onto your hard drive and burn them onto CDs. Plus, unlike Napster, the music available is both licensed and legal. Also, the quality is better.

Sash and I gave MSN music a try, going for the group, 'Cake.' When we type in 'Cake' and click, we are offered the chance to "Get more information on the artist 'Cake', "view SoundsLike Artists," or "play a SoundsLike Artist based on this artist." Sash clicked on the information option, which gave us a full bio, plus a list of albums.

MSN music has another cool feature. You can find music from your favorite artist to fit your mood: angry or trippy, quirky or happy, rockin', sad or soothing. You can also search favorite artist's works by style, tempo, vocals, and several other categories. And, it includes that "SoundsLike" feature that will bring up artists you don't know but who you might like. Sash liked this best. ("Trippy?")

Like most MSN products, you'll need to register for their free "Passport" to use the service to play radio music and save your favorites for later.

A few other notes from the Sasha music files: one great Internet music resource where he likes to find the history of music is artist fan pages. As a big Beatles fan who discovered the boys only recently, he directed me to a few large sites where a modern teen can unearth archeological clues about the Fab Four. And as a musician (sax and keyboard), he also recommends Midi, which Sash calls a sort of "piano roll" of music. Among its other features, Midi interfaces with other electronic instruments—like a keyboard—and provides information about the notes to change sounds, master volume, and even how long to sustain the note. (For a fuller explanation, go to **www.midi.com/**).

Another note on the music scene: last time we went to a concert (Richard Thompson, one of my faves), I headed home, punched up his fan site and, to my amazement, found backstage photos of Richard, his son Teddy, and the rest of the band already on the Web. A nice addition to a concert experience for aged—and not so aged—groupies.

Last tip to clueless parents: did you know lots of CDs now include computer links? For example, the popular "Oh Brother, Where Art Thou?" disc includes screen savers from the movie.

Talk the Talk

MP3: A format for recording and compressing music into almost CD quality. The compression makes it possible for files to be traded from one computer user to another over the Internet. Without it, music files would be much too big to transmit—even for those with DSL and cable modem connections.

Streaming Audio/Streaming Video: A technology that permits the simultaneous transmission and presentation of audio or video on your computer. With Streaming audio and video, you don't need to wait for the entire file to download before playing it.

Peer-to-peer: A decentralized way of exchanging files, done among individual PC's.

Streaming Audio and Video

Despite questionable quality as yet, streaming audio and video combinations are popping up online. Many are directed at teens or young adults, with popular movie stars, members of rock bands, and even live broadcasts of concerts or other events appearing at scheduled times.

To access streaming audio and video, you'll need to download a set of "plug-ins" such as Real Player, Microsoft Windows Media Player, and Quick Time. Plug-ins are software programs that add playing capabilities to your browser program. Once they're installed, you can play audio samples and view video clips at your computer.

Plug-ins enable streaming of video and audio. In the days before streaming, before you could see video clips or listen to audio from the Internet, you had to download the audio or video file to your computer. Only when the entire file was on the hard drive could you play it. The download could take several minutes or even hours. Streaming means that video or audio clips start playing as soon as they arrive—no need to fully download the piece first. (To find plug-ins, go to Live @, **www.live-at.com/index.html**.)

Home page of Live @, a broadcast audio and video service.

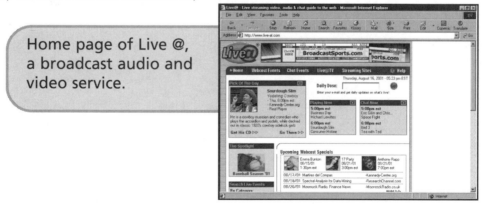

Online Auctions

By now everyone has heard of somebody who bought or sold something fabulous or useless on e-Bay, one of the popular online auctions. Personally, the only thing I ever tried to sell was a Sponge Bob Square pants doll (from Nicktoons) before the ultimate square became popular. (I had received it as a gift and no one wanted it, not even on e-Bay.) Sash, a jazz fan, has bought some excellent albums using e-Bay, and his friends use it as well.

E-Zines and Web Pages

While younger kids might be posting baseball Little League scores or artwork on their Web pages, a quick survey of teen Web pages shows a wide variety of self-expression and self-revelation. There are thousands out there. Many are constructed on homebuilding sites like gURL, Lycos, Bolt, Yahoo!Geocities, or ChickClick. Or they can be created independently, then linked to sites such as "Shut Up You're Only 16!" (**www.envy.nu/antigrrrl/ring**). Many contain poetry, photographs, drawings, animations, and diaries of daily life, which range from the most mundane observations of what they ate that day to rants about everything from current affairs to family life. To maintain their privacy, most are identified by nicknames or only a first name. Many teen "web rings"—associations of sites that are linked to one another usually by topic—ban banner ads on included sites.

E-zines can be similar to teen mags on the newsstand, with a concentration on looks and clothes. A search of the Web, however, convinced me that some of the most interesting 'zines (and home pages) are being created, interestingly enough, by teen girls. While there are plenty of "hearts and flowers" type pages, a number of young women seem to be using the Web to rail against the perky, pretty, vacuous image put forth in commercial media of boy-crazed teen girls. Many of the homemade e-zines and Web pages are smart, sassy places where girls gather, talk, and read about things that interest them, which sometimes, but not always, includes boys.

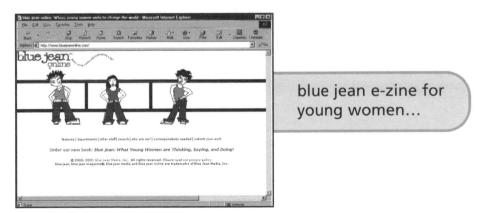

blue jean e-zine for young women...

In a recent article for "The Nation", writer and Web designer Bronwyn Garrity says the "bodiless" sensation of writing online can offer young girls a chance to develop a self free from society's fixation on female appearance. For this reason, many young women deliberately choose not to put their pictures on their sites. Or, as one young Web editor says, "I want a person to be able to look past the outside and realize that there is an opinionated, intelligent, creative young woman behind the pretty face."

Part of the reason for this exploration and explosion of girls' sites, has to do with what Suler calls the online "disinhibition effect"—that people open up a bit more in the "faceless world of text communication."

"Unfortunately, our culture and school system sometimes place pressure on teen girls to assume the traditional 'passive female' stereotype, while males are encouraged to assert themselves. Girls want to express and assert themselves too, and the online world—which doesn't contain the same social pressures as the offline world—gives them a place to do it."

Among the e-zines you might want to explore:

→ purple pajamas (**www.purplepjs.com**), an e-zine designed to let girls "discuss their views about current events and other topics of interest." Girls contribute material to the site, chat, and "get as silly or serious as they want in our discussion forums." The editors note that "Participation is welcome even if your writing skills aren't the greatest. We're more interested in sincerity and passion than in grammar or spelling."

→ bluejean (**www.bluejeanmedia.com**), "dedicated to empowering young women to create their own media," is produced and written by young women around the world. Bluejean rose from "blue jean" magazine, which showcased young women writers, poets, and artists and as an alternative to the glamour and beauty magazines targeting young women.

→ gurl (**www.gurl.com**), a slickly produced site with a refreshingly alternative take on the world. Recent sections include 'dead women you should know about' and a 'zit popping game.' A nice mix of the serious and the seriously-in-need–of-deflating fill these pages. Great cartoons.

→ react.com (**www.react.com**) is an e-zine billed as a place where "teens make and report the news." Not for girls only.

→ planetgirl.com (**www.planetgirl.com/**) has a portal where you can access home-made Web pages.

What Do Kids Do Online?

Send or read e-mail 92%
Surf the Web for fun..84%
Visit an entertainment site 83%
Send an instant message..74%
Look for info on hobbies 69%
Get news..68%
Play or download a game 66%
Research a product or service before buying it..............66%
Listen to music online..59%
Visit a chat room..55%
Download music files..53%
Check sports stores 47%
Visit a site for a club or team that they are a member of ...39%
Express opinions online 38%
Buy something...31%
Visit sites for trading or selling 31%
Look for health information..26%
Create a Web page..24%
Look for information about something that is hard to talk about 18%

(Source, Pew Internet Study, **www.pewinternet.org**)

Tracking Teens

These are among the findings in a new report from the Pew Internet & American Life Project called "Teenage Life Online: The rise of the instant-message generation and the Internet's impact on friendships and family relationships." The results are based on a phone survey of 754 teenagers and 754 of their parents by Princeton Survey Research Associates and a week-long online discussion group conducted in association with the research firm Greenfield Online.

→ **Seventeen million youths** between ages 12 and 17 or about three quarters of the teen population, use the Internet.

→ **About half of these teens** say their use of the Internet improves their relationships with their friends; 32% say it helps them make new friends.

→ **Almost two-thirds of online teens** say they think use of the Internet takes away from the time young people spend with their families.

→ **Thirteen million of these teenagers,** 74% of those with Internet access, have used instant messaging. While most instant messages are innocuous chit-chat, many are socially potent. More than a third of teens use IM to say things they don't want to say in face-to-face conversations with their peers. Almost a fifth (17%) have used IM to ask someone out, and more than a tenth (13%) have used IM to break up with someone.

→ **About a quarter of teens using e-mail**, instant messaging, or chat rooms exchange passwords as a sign of trust.

→ **Over half of parents worry that strangers will contact their children online.** These worries are well grounded. Close to 60% of teens have received an instant message or an e-mail from a stranger, and 50% report e-mailing or instant messaging with someone they have not met before. Despite this, teens themselves are not particularly worried about strangers online, with 52% saying they do not worry at all about being contacted.

→ **15% percent of online teens and 25% of older boys online have lied about their age to access a Web site.** This is one indication of how many teens have accessed online pornography.

→ **A quarter of the teens** surveyed say the Internet helps them get information about things that are hard to talk to other people about.

→ **87% percent of parents** believe the Internet helps their children in school; 78% of online teens agree.

(Source, Pew Internet Study, **www.pewinternet.org**)

Get Streaming!

Shazmo.com offers links to everything from Congressional coverage to Jessica Alba—all in streaming video and audio, **www.shazmo.com**

Cartoons, Abbott & Costello and the newest in claymation can be located using the Streaming Video and Movie Directory at **www.netbored.com/video.htm**.

Budding film makers, game designers, or Web animators will want to check out Atom Films **www.atomfilms.com** the 'big tuna of online films' according to the Chicago Tribune.

Need a reason to spend more time sitting before your PC? Grab some popcorn and head for CinemaNow **www.cinemanow.com** where full length movies are streamed for free. Or, if it's small screen you crave, head to LikeTelevision **http://tesla.liketelevision.com** where you can catch up on Johnny Carson, Shirley Temple, and other stars of yore.

Entertainment 101

Lots of teens use the Net as a break after a hard day and night of schoolwork. Some always popular sites while waiting for those IM buddies to come online:

Mighty Big TV (**www.mightybigtv.com**) is billed as Television Without Pity, and they mean it. Watch their critics rip into The Real World, Ally McBeal, and everything else they can get their claws into. Better than the real thing...

ESPN.com (**http://espn.go.com**): Enough sports and statistics to keep sports fans cheering. And don't forget the X-factor at EXPN.com (**http://expn.go.com**).

Salon (**www.salon.com**) and Slate (**www.slate.com**), are two online magazines with attitude, smarts, and a wide appetite for news and alternative views of the arts, business, technology, politics, sports, and beyond.

Got Junk?

Selling stuff online, from the fabulous to the ridiculous, is fueled not only by Moms and Dads, but teen collectors looking for awesome vinyl, retro clothes, and that perfect lava lamp. Start you search at ebay, **www.ebay.com**, but yahoo! (**http://auctions.yahoo.com**) and amazon.com (**www.amazon.com**) also host good auctions. Of course, there's always Sothebys (**www.sothebys.com**) and Christies (**www.christies.com**) for those who like to dream.

Get IM

Microsoft Messenger ....**http://messenger.msn.com**
AOL Instant Messenger (AIM) ....**www.aol.com/aim/home.html**
Yahoo! Messenger ....**http://messenger.yahoo.com**
Jabber ....**www.jabbercentral.com**

What You Need

To receive sounds online, in addition to your trusty computer and online hookup, you'll also need speakers and a sound card. And if you have a hankering to make your own—a microphone is nice.

Selling It

Chapter 9

Selling It

I love Harry Potter. More to the point, Noah loves Harry Potter. In the last seven months, he has read, re-read and re-re-read the four books. And like any red-blooded American Muggle, he waits for the next book, movie, toy, puzzle, wizard hat…well, you get the idea.

I know this, my husband knows this, his older brother knows this, and Warner Bros. Movie studio—the studio engaged in producing the Harry Potter films—knows this. How?

 Because Noah, along with millions upon millions of other children and teens and adults, has logged on at the Harry Potter site (**http://harrypotter.warner-bros.com/home.html**), home of *The Daily Prophet*, the wizards' must-read newspaper. At this charmed site, wizard wanna-bes can pick up a personalized magic wand at Diagon Alley, get sorted by the infamous Sorting Hat into a Hogwarts house, and practice their budding Quidditch skills at Chaser Practice. All in all, it's a fun and exciting extension for Harry's many fans.

Oh, and by the way, did I mention that the site also features trailers from the Harry Potter movie? Along with a helpful store where you can purchase Harry Potter games, toys, and collectibles? And now that my son Noah has logged onto the site (using my e-mail address), I've begun to receive e-mails breathlessly entitled "The Latest from Hogwarts" that give our family a chance to sign the "what is sure to be the BIGGEST birthday card ever" for the tragically gifted Harry?

Let me repeat: I love Harry Potter. Noah loves Harry Potter. So what is wrong with this picture? Warner Bros. is entitled, after all, to sell and advertise their product, a product that Noah enjoys. The site is well designed and artful, the games fun and to the point. With my permission, Noah entered his name and e-mail address to join the site.

Stickiness

If you find yourself—or your child—returning again and again to a certain site, then for you—and maybe for others—that's a 'sticky' site. Advertisers and Web masters love sticky sites, although what brings you and your kids back for more isn't always clear. Crowd pleasers, however, often include sites with regularly updated content, ongoing contests, streaming video, games, and lots of links that lead to other places within the same site.

But here is the catch: Harry Potter is not designated as a children's site. This means that, unlike "kids' sites," the information Warner Bros. gathers from Harry Potter pages (according to the Privacy Policy attached to the site), can be used to—among other things—fulfill Noah's requests for products, fulfill a request for a newsletter, and offer you "other products or services which we feel may be of interest to you." Information can also be used to "improve the design of our site and to personalize the Internet experience." While taking appropriate measures to protect and safeguard against unauthorized disclosures of information, there are also times when it may disclose personally identifiable information to companies whose practices are not covered by their privacy policy—other marketers, magazine publishers, retailers, participatory databases, and non-profit organizations "that want to market products or services to you." If you don't want your information going to such groups, you can 'opt out' by notifying the webmaster of the site.

For those not schooled in legalese—and that includes me—what this means is that personal information and not-so-personal information (how many times you go to the site, which pages you visit most, etc.) will be stored in databases, or on cookies, text files that are picked up by your computer browser and stored on your hard drive, or both. But, as pointed out by one computer expert, if you do decide to opt out of the cookie business, you are then counted as one of those who have opted out of cookies altogether, and won't be able to take advantage of the benefits cookies can offer.

To repeat: what's wrong with this picture? Well, nothing really. Adults do read the Harry Potter series. And this is an adult site. But Harry Potter—a children's book series—is read by my nine-year-old, along with tons of other third-graders enamored of Harry Potter who log onto this site. And, unless Noah specifically opts out of the normal practice of the site's stated privacy policy, his movements online will be tracked, targeted, and monitored by Time-Warner, one of the largest communications companies on the planet.

Does all of this information collecting and distributing necessarily mean that you shouldn't let your kids explore the Web? Or voyage to any commercial sites?

Of course not. But you should pay close attention to the kinds of personal information being requested by sites that your kids visit and to what the sites plan to do with this information. For while advertisers and target marketing companies have every right to promote their goods, you have every right to ascertain that your kids' interests and privacy rights are protected.

Aside from privacy issues, many kids' sites contain ads. The choice for many Web companies, says Idit Harel of MaMaMedia, is pretty simple: either carry ads and stay solvent or charge for a kids' educational and game site service. Having chosen to put ads on the site, Harel's company tries to keep them minimal, and to label them clearly. If kids leave, they are alerted—as they are at Nickolodeon.com—that they are leaving the site. "It was very important to us to present our materials to kids around the world in the same format, and that they did not have to pay." And while Harel says she's working on ways to make the site ad free, for the moment, it's the best solution.

"We live in a commercial world," she says.

Apart from monitoring your child's computer travels as they hit sites with ads and reading a site's privacy policy with care, your best defense against exploitation of marketers is a good dose of media literacy, says Kyle Peck, Ph.D, professor of Education and Technology at Penn State University. "Teach kids what ads are and what they are for. If kids have a goal while online and think it's important, they won't bother to click on that banner ad because it will take them away from that goal."

Cookies

A cookie is a string of information that a Web site sends to your hard disk each time you visit the site. Cookies can personalize Web pages you visit, aid in online sales, or track demographics or popular links. Cookies are commonly used to rotate and customize banner ads based on information you've provided the Web sites.

While most experts see no danger in cookies, others find the collection and tracking process a threat to individual privacy. While you may be o.k. with a site tracking your movements, you may be less happy to know that they can also track your children's movements and preferences. Many people argue that the "invisible" gathering of information done by cookies—without your permission—is unethical, particularly when the data is sold to a third party.

For more about cookies, go to "Cookie Central" at **www.cookiecentral.com**, a site devoted to all you ever wanted to know about cookies. To quote the Unofficial Cookie FAQ (also found on the site), "If you can't find your answers there, one may not exist."

What is COPPA?

To help prevent marketers from abusing personal information collected from children on designated kids sites and to put parents in charge of what information is collected from their kids online, on April 21, 1998, Congress passed the Children's Online Privacy Protection Act (COPPA). Enforced by the Federal Trade Commission (FTC), COPPA helps protect the basic privacy rights of children under 13 and their parents. It was passed because more and more Web site operators are collecting personal information from children without consulting parents. Prior to COPPA—which went into effect on April 21, 2000—many sites were making money by selling marketing and demographic information gathered from kids' sites. (To learn more about COPPA go to **www.ftc.gov/kidzprivacy**.)

COPPA applies to Web sites directed at children and to "general audience" sites that are aware that kids under 13 are using their site. Under COPPA provisions:

➔ **Every site must link to a clear and comprehensive privacy policy** that explains how information collected on the site will be used and whether it will be forwarded to advertisers or to any other parties.

➔ **Before a site collects personal information from your child**, it must obtain verifiable parental consent. Even if you've given consent, however, you can also refuse to have the information passed on to a third party.

➔ **Parents have the right to revoke any information given by a child to a Web site**, and to have that information deleted from the site.

➔ **Site operators must maintain the "confidentiality, security, and integrity"** of any information collected from children.

➔ **Kids can't be prohibited from participating in an online activity** by requiring them to provide more personal information than is reasonably necessary to participate in that activity.

Brand Loyalty

Brand loyalty is important for teens. But unlike kids, teens have more sophistication when it comes to overt marketing, so Web sites often include more subversive brand content. One example are teen zines directed to girls such as Alloy (**www.alloy.com**) or Chickclick (**www.chickclick.com**), where ads merge with content. A feature on improving your body image, for example, may be flanked by little sidebars of makeup firms or DVDs related to the topic.

Kid's privacy protection discussion at the COPPA site.

How well is COPPA working overall? An examination of 153 children's commercial Web sites at the law's one-year anniversary by the Center for Media Education (CME) shows that COPPA appears to have significantly affected many of their marketing and business practices. The study reveals that more sites limit the type and amount of personal information they collect as a requirement for children to use a Web site, and more sites post privacy policies (although a majority do not display them as the required "clear and prominent" link). However, the survey also notes that most sites requiring parental consent before collecting a child's personal data have yet to do so properly. And that in their attempt to restrict children under age 13 from entering personal information, some Web sites use methods that might encourage kids to simply lie about their age.

To test the last proposition, Noah and I logged onto a number of commercial kids' Web sites and found it was a simple manner of plugging in a falsified birthdate to gain entrance to the site. Sites that require parents to call a 1-800 number or to mail in signed permission were, understandably, more resistant to our subterfuge.

If you think a kids' Web site is not complying with COPPA, you can contact your State Attorney General or notify the Federal Trade Commission:

Federal Trade Commission Consumer Response Center
Room 130
600 Pennsylvania Ave. NW
Washington, DC 20580

Or, you can contact them at their web site, **www.ftc.gov** or call toll-free 1-877-FTC-HELP (1-877-382-4357).

Give COPPA a Helping Hand

"Kids are smart," says Michael Antecol, a wired youth analyst at Forrester, Inc., a research firm specializing in Internet issues. "If they want to see something, they will."

Since this seems true to this Mom, the FTC recommends going over the following points with your children:

→ **Never give out your last name**, your home address, or phone number on chat rooms, bulletin boards or to online pen pals.

→ **Don't tell other kids your screen name**, user ID, or password.

→ **Look at a Web site's Privacy Policy** to see how the site uses information you give to them.

→ **Go online with your parents** and talk to them about the sites you visit.

→ **Talk about a site's Privacy Policy** with your parents so you—and they—understand what personal information the site collects and how it handles it.

→ **Web sites must get your parent's permission** before they collect personal information from you.

→ **If a Web site has information about you** that your parents don't want them to have, your parents can ask the Web site to erase or delete the information.

→ **Sites are not supposed to collect more information than they need about you** for the activity you want to participate in. You should be able to participate or play in any activity online without having to give any information about yourself.

→ **If a site makes you feel uncomfortable** or asks for more information than you want to share, leave the site.

I'd add one practical point to the FTC recommendations. Be sure your very young child knows how to use the back and forward buttons to get out of a site. If they find themselves "lost" in a realm of pop-up or 'sticky' ads (named because they're tough to get away from), teach your kids to back out of the site, or to close the browser and begin again.

Targets: Your Kids & Teens

So why do large corporations like Time-Warner, Nickelodeon, and Nintendo want your kids' personal information in the first place? This part is a no-brainer: kids influence how families' spend their money in a very big way, particularly teenagers. Jupiter Communications reports that in 2000, teens spent $41 billion. Of that figure, $4.1 billion went to "Web influenced purchases" while $500 million went to direct purchases online.

Figures like this get the attention of marketers and advertisers. While many parents and privacy groups worry about the broad swath of consumerism which seems ever present on kids' and teen sites on the Web, to marketers it's a 'virtual' gold mine. After all, says James McNeal, author of *The Kids Market: Myths and Realities*, since children eventually grow up to be the prime target market, "it makes sense to get their attention when they are young."

If kids are over 13—out of COPPA range—all the better, since marketers can then dream up sites that not only sell products, but also freely employ those cookies and databases to track the demographics and desires of their teen customers. Information gathered by teen sites can also be sold to other markets: a double bonanza.

Extra Credit

The sites below provide food for thought when it comes to ads and kids.

Advertising Rules for Kids

www.media-awareness.ca/eng/med/class/teamedia/adrls2.htm - An interesting list of rules for Canadian broadcasters when advertising to children.

Children, Youth & Advertising

http://interact.uoregon.edu/MediaLit/FA/MLadvertchild.html -A long list of resources on how kids are often sold more than products.

Commercial Alert

www.commercialalert.org/zapme/index.html - Reactions to a corporate initiative to give free computers to schools in exchange for exposing students to banner ads and the collection of demographic information.

Center for the Analysis of Commercialism in Education
(University of Wisconsin - Milwaukee)

www.schoolcommercialism.org/-CACE conducts research, disseminates information, and helps facilitate a dialogue between the education community, policy makers, and the public-at-large about commercial activities in the schools. CACE is the only national academic research center dedicated to this topic, and their site contains a list of links that relate to advertising in education.

(Thanks to Laura Fokkena.)

Tricks of the Trade

In 1996, the Center for Media Education published an influential report entitled "Web of Deception: Threats to Children of Online Marketing," that analyzed various marketing techniques directed at children. While some of the most egregious practices have been addressed by COPPA, others still merit consideration. (The complete report can be found at **www.cme.org**.)

Flow

A primary objection by critics to the onslaught of online marketing to kids resides in the interactive nature of the Web. Kids are particularly subject to the lure of what marketers have dubbed the "flow state"—a condition where Web travelers effortlessly and sometimes mindlessly move from one frame of the Web to the next, clicking seamlessly from an ad to a noncommercial site to a commercially sponsored game to an ad, and so on. As kids do this, the lines between advertising content and other subject matter can become increasingly blurred.

Games

While many kids' television programs take advantage of marketing products related to content—Pokémon and his many cards and plush pals; Sesame Street and Tickle-Me-Elmo, to name but two—commercial Web sites promoting brands take this one step further by designing interactive games that blatantly advertise brands.

One of Noah's favorite destinations, for example, is Candystand.com (**www.candystand.com/**), sponsored by the Lifesavers Company. Entering the site, we're swept into a tempting display of goodies manufactured by the company. Along with invitations to play games on the site—our true destination once we get past the ad copy—there are promotions for games (COPPA permits kids to provide a "one time only e-mail for games" without parental consent), opportunities to win prizes from Sony, and an icon to click to enter Nabisco World, another game site.

If you can keep your focus on your goal—in our case to play golf on this site—you can click from here into a very well-designed miniature golf game. But don't think you've left the sweet motif behind: from the first to 18th link, each hole (another reference to the brand?) cheerily features representations of life-savers, cremesavers, and various other product placements in its core design.

Let's be clear. It's a fun site. Noah, accustomed (as your child may be) to commercial to tie-ins to games he plays, television shows and cartoons he watches, and even cereal boxes he reads, he claims he "barely notices the ads." This may be true. But don't forget that sophisticated marketing went into this site, marketing designed to attract and instill brand loyalty as your child plays an innocent game of putt-putt golf. The message is clear, Lifesavers = fun, good times, pleasure, and hopefully purchases down the road. The one-on-one interactivity that makes the game exciting also creates a bond that your child may or may not be sophisticated enough to evaluate and understand. Talk to them about it.

Content or Ads?

When kids log on to the games page of Nick.com, the Web site of the Nickelodeon television network, one of the first things they are likely to encounter is a banner ad that reads: "You're a player? Choose a game." Game choices include the Honeycomb Craver Course, Lunchables Scooter Challenge, Climb Mt. Mac & Cheese, and KOOL-AID Wakeboarding. A click of the mouse takes them not to Nick.com's games page, but to a site run by Kraft Foods. The banner is a byproduct of the new emphasis among consumer marketers to use branded online games as a tool to raise product awareness. Nick.com also has branded games on the site, called "Advertoys."

Challenges abound here. In addition to the one-on-one enticement of free gaming, these sites also provide confusion in their graphics. Since the site design and the design of the banner ad is similar—fluorescent colors, quirky kid friendly typeface, and familiar jargon—"You're a player?"—kids can hit the ad and move into Kraft World without fully understanding what makes this different from a content area.

Join up

Ad agencies and target marketers know that kids of any age like to be part of something. To glom onto this desire, many sites offer prizes, "kid kash," points and the like to collect items on the site so they can join the club. Newsletters sent to kids (like the Harry Potter one cited above) also encourage this community. Remember that if you send an e-mail from a site, you've given them your e-mail plus the e-mail of a friend—a new contact for the site's sponsors.

Star Power

Celebrities can increase purchases. A new entrant on the scene is Britney ("Oops, I Did it Again") Spears at **www.britneyspears.com**. While her "Official Fan Site" includes plenty of pictures, e-mail cards, and FAQs about the popular singer, it also includes a connection to a Britney shop, where young fans can pick up items associated in some way with their fave rave. I went on the site (without Noah, who is not exactly a fan) to check out what's offered. When I was there, products ranged from Nokia phones to cheap temporary tattoos. (Note: Preteens and teens have been targeted by a number of marketers as the "about to explode" audience for cell phones; apparently the U.S. has fallen far beyond European and Japanese consumers in this area.)

More disturbing to me than the products was the layout of the site. Options along the left side of the screen in very small type offer free chances for visitors to interact with fellow fans and to gather Britney news. But these opportunities are given reduced play compared to the upper right hand corner bulletin that announces in large type: "STORE."

If you want to see how content and advertisements blend, simply pick one of your child's favorite brands: Pepsi, Nike, Hershey, or Game Boy. Take a hard look. Can your child tell the difference between content and come-ons?

The Official Britney
Spears site.

Web Purchases

Marketers are clear: the only thing between a child or teen and purchases online is access to a credit card.

Since most kids and teens don't have their own credit card accounts, parents retain control over this method. But companies have come up with a way around this barrier: "alternative cash" systems where adults deposit funds into debit cards that can be used like credit-cards online. Among the most popular are Rocketcash.com, Flooz.com, and PayPal.com. On these sites, kids can have parents deposit cash into debit cards that can be used 'like credit-cards.' Some cards claim to include a code on the card that will prevent kids from buying alcohol, tobacco, or other restricted products.

Catching onto this trend, branded products also link to these cash alternatives. For example, a recent Sprite promotion offers Rocketcash dollars for "Sprite points" collected from cans and bottles.

These cards can be a convenient way for kids to shop online while placing limits on spending (they can't go over the funds available on the card). Individual companies, like Gap, also offer this service. In addition to their ease, however, parents might want to realize that using such cards provide another way for teenagers' purchases to be tracked by marketers and advertisers online. Credit card companies and banks are notorious for selling such information.

Rocketcash: one of several alternative payment methods offered for teens and others to use online.

Blocking Ads

One answer to direct Web advertising is to employ ad-blocking software that can erase banner ads, pop-up ads, and cookies that track your Web movements online.

Along with clearing your screen of advertisements, there are several other advantages to blocking ads. These include:

→ **Speed.** When you reduce the wait for banner ads to load, your browsing becomes much faster.

→ **Less Distraction.** Moving or animated banner ads cut into your focus. Without them, it's easy to concentrate.

→ **More privacy.** Cookies and ad networks track your Web movements and may invade your actual identity. Without ads, they have no way to monitor personal information or your 'click-path' on the Web. (This goes, of course, for the privacy of your children and teens as well.)

To explore issues surrounding blocking ads (and spam) head for a comprehensive discussion at Junkbusters (**www.junkbusters.com**). Here you can download the Internet Junkbuster Proxy that will disable cookies and block ads, as well as a link to the similar but newer Guidescope (**www.guidescope.com**) blocking software.

A number of other companies offer ad-blocking software. They include Adkiller (**www.adkiller.com**), muffin (**http://muffin.doit.org**), and WebWasher (**www.webwasher.com**).

Along with banner ads, some programs also rid your screen of pesky pop-up ads. If you're interested in zapping these critters, you can investigate Ad Subtract Pro (**www.adsubtract.com**) and Pop Not (**www.hdsoft.com/popnot**).

And last but not least, while most ad-blocking software blocks cookies, you can opt out of Doubleclick—one of the advertising agencies that track your movements online—by heading for **www.doubleclick.com**.

Projects: Teaching Kids Media Literacy

Going online with your children and helping them to recognize when and how they are being solicited by marketers is the best way to deal with online ads. Point out when a site aims personalized messages to them, by making Web site entertainment appear like education, or by encouraging them to click on banners or icons that will take them to advertising pages.

→ **What's The Message?** Can your child identify the difference between content and commercials? Look up sites that advertise products that your kids like or already own and ask whether the information on the site is aimed at educating them or selling to them. Check out American Girl (**www.americangirl.com),** Barbie (**www.barbie.com**), or Hot Wheels (**www.hot-wheels.com**) or your kids' favorites.

→ **Count the Ads.** Have your child go onto the Scholastic for Kids (**www.scholastic.com**) to count the ads. Talk about how they might have missed some of the ads on the site. Then compare this with ads that are identified, such as Mama Media (**www.MaMaMedia.com**). Among questions suggested by Education World to ask your child about ads are: How did you find ads? What clues do you use? Do you think all kids' sites should have identification on ads? Why or why not?

→ **Capturing Kids' Attention.** Look at different types of commercial and noncommercial sites to see if they're educational, recreational, commercial, or a combination. Try Nintendo (**www.nintendo.com**), the Olympic Games site (**www.olympic.com**), the PBS Kids (**www.pbskids.org**), and The Yuckiest Site on the Net (**www.yucky.kids.discovery.com**). How do ads get kids attention? Why do kid's sites often offer games, collectibles, bright colors, cool vocabulary, or all of the above? What about ads that 'pop-up,' interrupting play?

→ **Dinnertime with teens.** Advertising and its effects can provide an eye opening dinner time discussion. According to The Center for a New American Dream (**http://www.new-dream.org/campaign/kids/facts.html**), children's spending has doubled every 10 years for three decades, then tripled in the 1990's. Advertisers now spend 20 times more on marketing to kids than they did just ten years ago. One study shows that high school students are very resistant to the idea that kids in a Pepsi commercial are in fact paid actors rather than 'real kids,' and often believe that athletes paid corporations to star in TV ads, not the other way around (**http://www.ibiblio.org/stayfree/archives/13/manipulated.html**).

→ **What's the solution?** Ads pay the way for some sites on the Web. If your children and teens find them annoying, can they think of ways to fund their favorite pages? Would they rather pay a fee for the services they use, like a magazine subscription? Would you? What if ads only appeared on one page of the site? Or only at the entrance? What if certain types of ads—like pop-ups—were banned?

Protecting
Kids
Online
Chapter 10

Protecting Kids Online

Not so long ago, I sat by Noah's side while he showed me a new online game. It was a version of hangman, played with seven other participants, each of whom took turns in a counterclockwise progression. At first sight, it looked fun, innocent, and perfectly age appropriate, until I noticed that while my son took his turn, the other seven players engaged in what could only be described as stunningly lewd conversation. I leaned forward.

"Noah?" I asked. "What's all this?"

"Oh, that," he said. "Don't sweat it, Mom. It's only noise."

By now, every parent has read stories about the dangers lurking for children on the Internet. For all the wonderful worlds of learning and entertainment that the Internet can bring into kids' lives, here was the well-publicized downside of technology sitting in my little boy's bedroom.

What to do? To answer that question, you need to look at your own child and you're parenting style. Quite frankly, it helps to look at this as a parenting issue rather than a technological one. What disturbs one child may not bother the next. Every parent has different standards about what is "appropriate" for their children that can even vary from brother to sister or brother to brother.

You also need to assess your child's maturity when it comes to operating online. Some kids can 'brush off' the occasional offensive remark or picture that pops up while they're online, while others may feel threatened.

These are not simple issues. The World Wide Web, after all, was not designed primarily for children and it does contain a great deal of "adults-only" content. There are people who prey on children online in chat rooms, on discussion boards, through e-mail, sometimes for 'fun,' sometimes for less understandable reasons.

But at the same time, much of this danger has been overblown.

Take the issue of online predators. Despite wide media coverage, child molestation or kidnapping resulting from online stalking is highly unlikely. According to the 2001 Pew Internet Study, the greatest risk is that "a child might run into a mean, obnoxious, or angry person in a chat area or newsgroup." The solution? Ignore the intruder, get off line, report them to the service or your ISP, and maybe most importantly, tell you, the parent.

"Parents who understand the Internet and monitor the time that they want a child to spend online offer the best protection for kids going online," says Richard Sherman, Ph.D, a psychologist specializing in children and Internet issues. Sherman emphasises that each child is different, and that how the Internet will be used depends on the families' needs and policies. But overall, he says, "Kids need appropriate monitoring by parents at home to prevent inappropriate behavior online."

"The Internet is an incredible resource of information for adults and children," says Sherman. "But if parents don't understand how to use it, they shouldn't get a child access."

When it comes to protecting your child from inappropriate sexual or hateful material on the Internet, it may not be possible. Or even desirable. The Internet, as a reflection of the world, contains all the diversity—desirable and undesirable—that the world contains.

If you think of the Internet as a reflection of the world, you can prepare your child in much the same way you do before you send them to a public playground. Don't talk to strangers. Don't reveal personal information to people you don't know. If someone bothers you, run away and tell Mom or Dad or another responsible adult.

To help you arrive at an appropriate policy for your family, you need to be aware of the risks and some common sense ways to approach them. For some parents, installing a Web filter or subscribing to an Internet Service Provider that blocks certain sites may be a partial answer. In this chapter, we'll address what your kids need to know before they go online, family pledges on Internet policy at home, and the pros and cons of filtering information.

Guidelines for Cyber Kids

Like sending your child into any public arena, heading onto cyberspace poses certain risks. Kids can face intruders in kids' chat rooms, inappropriate behavior from adults or even other kids online, and temptations like gambling games. But as in any other "real world" situation, kids have choices in cyberspace on how to deal with dangers.

Knowing the particular risks of online life is the first step to helping insure your kids' safety. The more you know, the more you can anticipate what they'll face. This means spending time with your child online, as well as asking your child regularly about their online "friends," and about any interesting sites they've recently visited. As in any other parenting situation, being on top of the situation—knowing where your child is and what they're doing—will pay off both in bringing you closer and making you, and your child, feel more secure about sharing any problems they might encounter online.

Talk to them about some of the things, good and bad, they find online. Talk with your kids about what dangers you, and they, see online. If you haven't been online much, particularly in chat rooms or Instant Messaging, you might get some ideas from them about times or places they feel uncomfortable. Basically, there is no substitute for sitting beside your child and helping them find appropriate sites to explore.

What are the risks for kids online?

Password Protection

Sometimes it's not enough to tell your kids not to give out a password. To help up your level of security, help kids choose passwords with these dos and don'ts from security experts:

→ Do go for a random mix of letters and numbers. The scramble seems harder for crooks to crack.

→ Do try to find a word that's not in the dictionary, since programs exist that can go through and test your entry.

→ Don't use pet names, birthdays, telephone numbers, family names, obscene words, cartoon characters, actors' names, or movies.

Loss of Privacy

Teach kids that just because someone asks them for personal information, they don't have to respond. Ninety-nine percent of the time when people ask for your address or your hometown, it's an innocent request, but it's a bad idea to give them out freely. Even if it's simply a form to enter a site or talk to an animated cartoon figure, instruct kids that they must ask a grownup first.

When it comes to very young children, explain exactly what qualifies as personal information. Most kids understand not to give out their names and addresses, but let them know they shouldn't reveal their telephone numbers, zip codes, names of their school, their parents, sisters or brothers, hobbies, pet names, or anything else that is 'private.'

In addition, encourage your kids to pick gender neutral nicknames for chat rooms or game sites to avoid possible teasing or harassment. Instruct them never to send digital images of themselves online and to never, ever agree to meet anyone face-to-face that they meet online without informing you first.

Forms or direct requests for information aren't the only places where personal information can be revealed. Remind your kids that the Internet is an open forum, so that when they post a message or speak in a chat room, any one can read their words. Therefore, it's a good policy not to say or post anything online that they don't feel comfortable telling everyone.

Teach your child never to reveal an Internet or AOL password to anyone, even if the person claims to work for AOL or an Internet service provider. This includes friends.

When in doubt, remind them to come to you.

Strangers

Of all the dangers online, harassment by strangers—sexual, angry, or predatory by nature—appears to be the most common. Strangers may approach children via unsolicited e-mail, in chat rooms, on bulletin boards. Remind your children that they need not respond to angry or suggestive talk, and that if they are approached, they need to tell you.

Most people your kids will meet on the Internet are honest and interested in communicating in a truthful way. However, there are people who—for various reasons, including fun—assume other identities. For example, it's easy for an adult to pretend to be a child on the Net. While this doesn't mean that your children need to be suspicious of every person they meet online, if someone asks for pictures or seems too eager to have them move into a private chat room area or asks for inappropriate or personal information, be sure your kids know how to get out of that area and know that they need to inform you.

As a parent, try to get to know your child's friends on the Internet, just as you would their school pals.

Inappropriate Material

Stumbling on inappropriate sexual, violent, or hateful information online is extremely easy. Some Web sites and newsgroups contain information that advocates the use of drugs, tobacco, or alcohol. There are sites that allow people to gamble with real money or just "for fun." In some cases these sites may be operating legally in the jurisdiction where they are physically located, but it is generally illegal (and inappropriate) for minors to gamble regardless of where they are. It's even possible to find places on the Internet where you can learn to make bombs or obtain weapons.

Graphic or false information also arrives in unsolicited e-mail or spam. (GET RICH QUICK!!!CREDIT CARDS FOR FREE!!!) As adults, we know to delete such messages, but kids might be intrigued. Explain spam to kids as the junk mail it is and ask them not to open mail unless they see an address they recognize.

To help deal with this, show your child how to 'back out' using the forward or back button on your browser.

To help clarify the issue for your kids, make sure your children understand what sites you consider appropriate for them. What sorts of sites do you want them to visit? Are there any areas that are off limits?

Legal and Social Issues

Teach your kids to behave online as they would in any other public place. This means observing good netiquette, and avoiding being mean, rude, or inconsiderate when they're online.

Guidelines for Parents of Teens

Keeping tabs on younger kids (thirteen and under) online is admittedly easier than tracking teen use. After all, teens are more likely to have PCs in their bedrooms, often behind closed bedroom doors. Teenagers also tend to go online later in the evening to chat with friends on IM, and based on *Wired Youth*, a Forrester, Inc. 2001 study, have the "technical wherewithal to erase their tracks by erasing information about where they've visited from the history of their browsers."

Despite their technological skills and hormonal resistance to parenting, however, you need to talk to them about safe use of the Internet. It doesn't mean that they'll listen—it might be tough to find a teenage boy who hasn't been on a questionable adult site or two. But following a few basic rules can protect them from harassment online. And while you discuss some safe guidelines for online use, it's also a good (and often enlightening) idea to talk to your teen about his or her favorite Web sites, chat areas, and IM buddies.

Maintain Your Privacy

Keep your address, phone number, and other personal information off any personal Web sites or sites sponsored by a school or organization. If you want people to contact you, give an e-mail address.

Entering a Web site or anywhere else online means sacrificing some of your privacy. Remember that names and personal tidbits can end up in a database used by companies to track your purchases or simply sites you visit on the Net. In the worst case, the information could be used by criminals or for exploitation purposes.

If you're in any type of public forum, such as a chat room or a bulletin board, avoid giving out your full name, your mailing address, your telephone number, the name of your school, or any other information that could help someone determine your actual identity. The same applies to your family and friends.

Never reveal anything about other people that could possibly get them into trouble, and never give out your password to anyone, even friends.

→ **Trust your instincts.** If you're receiving harassing e-mail, don't write back. Report any e-mail that makes you feel uncomfortable or appears threatening to your Internet Service Provider. If you get such a message, don't respond— you may simply encourage the sender. Instead, show it to your parents or a trusted adult to see if there is anything you can do to make it stop.

→ **Be careful how you respond to e-mail** from people you don't know. Remember, the sender might not be who he or she seems to be. Never send a photograph of yourself or any personal information to someone you don't know. Also, e-mail can easily be copied and forwarded to others. So if you do send personal information to friends, be sure that they are willing to respect your privacy.

→ **Don't respond to spam mail** or mail from an address you don't recognize. By responding, you can encourage a person who may be sending inappropriate e-mail or inadvertently add your name to more spam lists. Show messages that contain graphic, violent, or illegal content to your parents and/or report them to your Internet Service Provider.

→ **Never, ever agree to meet an online acquaintance face-to-face.** For one, people who are online aren't always who they claim to be. If you want to meet someone, make sure you talk it over with your parents first. Meet in a public place—a restaurant or mall—that you know well, and never go alone.

More important than specific guidelines, perhaps, is to simply chat with your teen regularly about all of their activities, including their Internet ones.

"To kids, connecting to the computer means connecting to their culture," says Jon Katz, author of *Geeks* and a columnist for **www.slashdot.org**. "Let your kids know you respect what they're doing online. Ask them to show you what they're working on."

Family Contracts

Pulled between work, school, and after school commitments, it's often not possible to monitor a child's activities 24/7. But to achieve piece of mind on this sometimes tricky area, many parents establish a family contract and a safety pledge to cover their children's time online.

As Katz has noted, when it comes to how media is managed in a household, "There'll probably be as many different kinds of contracts as there are families." Katz has written about a comprehensive 'media contract' that permits responsible children and parents to thrash out a shared value system around media issues, in which a parent spells out how much Internet time they find appropriate, along with what obligations are expected from their child: chores, school performance, etc. At the same time, a child who meets these obligations, would spell out how much time she'd like to spend online. Along with that, she agrees to safety guidelines: alerting parents if she hits upon inappropriate sites, not giving out telephone numbers or home addresses to strangers, etc. "Access," he writes, "is granted as a right, but it's subject to some conditions." (To read Katz's "The Rights of Kids in the Digital Age" see **www.wired.com/ wired/archive/4.07_pr.html**.)

If you decide to draw up your own "social contract" for Internet use, be sure to tailor it to you and your children's needs and expectations. Among the areas you may want to cover:

→ What are your expectations for your children's Internet use? What about your kids' expectations? Do you want them to limit weeknight online time to research and homework and weekends for games and entertainment? How much time should be allotted for chat or IM? Do you want your younger children to use chat rooms at all?

→ What should a child do if she stumbles on a disturbing or inappropriate site? How about your teenagers?

→ How should kids handle unwanted spam mail? Do you want younger (under 13) kids to open their own e-mail accounts or should they share your address?

→ How much time do you want your child to spend online? What qualifies as "too much" use? What if you see your child is spending too much time online?

→ Will you be looking at the daily history of the browser to see where he's visited? Or is that an unthinkable violation of your child's privacy?

→ What happens if your child's grades slip or they begin to neglect their household chores? Will that affect Internet privileges?

Under ideal situations, these discussions would take place before your kids first log on. Yet even if you've missed that moment, talking these issues over with your children is a good idea anytime. The point isn't to scare or threaten them, but to educate them about what you see as safe and reasonable Internet use.

Safety Pledges

Along with a family contract on Internet use, you may also want to draw up a safety pledge that covers many of the guidelines above. You can find many examples of such pledges online, or you can draw up one on your own. Once you and your children have signed it, post it near the computer so kids have the provisions handy.

One of the best pledges has been composed by Larry Magid, Ph.D, a syndicated columnist specializing in technology issues for the Los Angeles Times and CBS News. (Go to **www.safekids.com/** and **www.safeteens.com** for comprehensive coverage of safety issues for kids and teens online.)

On the following pages are two sample pledges from the site:

The Ten Commandments for Computer Ethics

Most pledges try to protect kids from harm while online. In a bit of a reversal, Ramon C. Barquin of the Computer Ethics Institute in Washington, D.C., came up with a set of computer "commandments" that protect others from your (and your kids') time online. Moses might not have recognized them, but here goes:

1. Thou shalt not use a computer to harm other people.
2. Thou shalt not interfere with other people's computer work.
3. Thou shalt not snoop around in other people's files.
4. Thou shalt not use a computer to steal.
5. Thou shalt not use a computer to bear false witness.
6. Thou shalt not use or copy software for which you have not paid.
7. Thou shalt not use other people's computer resources without authorization.
8. Thou shalt not appropriate other people's intellectual output.
9. Thou shalt think about the social consequences of the program you write.
10. Thou shalt use a computer in ways that show consideration and respect.

Copyright: 1991 Computer Ethics Institute
Author: Dr. Ramson C. Barquin

Kids' Pledge

I will not give out personal information such as my address, telephone number, parents' work address/telephone number, or the name and location of my school without my parents' permission.

I will tell my parents right away if I come across any information that makes me feel uncomfortable.

I will never agree to get together with someone I 'meet' online without first checking with my parents. If my parents agree to the meeting, I will be sure that it is in a public place and bring my mother or father along.

I will never send a person my picture or anything else without first checking with my parents.

I will not respond to any messages that are mean or in any way make me feel uncomfortable. It is not my fault if I get a message like that. If I do, I will tell my parents right away so that they can contact the service provider.

I will talk with my parents so that we can set up rules for going online. We will decide upon the time of day that I can be online, the length of time I can be online, and appropriate areas for me to visit. I will not access other areas or break these rules without their permission

I will not give out my Internet password to anyone (even my best friends), other than my parents.

I will be a good online citizen and not do anything that hurts other people or is against the law.

I agree to the above

_____

Child sign here

I will help my child follow this agreement and will allow reasonable use of the Internet as long as these rules and other family rules are followed.

_____

Parent(s) sign here

Monitoring Internet use is a two way street. (And kids are likely to take your rules more seriously if you sign up as well.) In that spirit, a parents' contract is provided as well:

Parents' Pledge

I will get to know the services and Web.

I will set reasonable rules and guidelines for computer use by my children and will discuss these rules and post them near the computer as a reminder.

I'll remember to monitor their compliance with these rules, especially when it comes to the amount of time they spend on the computer and/or Web sites. If I don't know how to use them, I'll get my child to show me how.

I will not overreact if my child tells me about a problem he or she is having on the Internet. Instead, we'll work together to try to solve the problem and prevent it from happening again.

I promise not to use a PC or the Internet as an electronic babysitter.

I will help make the Internet a family activity and ask my child to help plan family events using the Internet.

I will try get to know my child's "online friends" just as I try get to know his or her other friends.

I agree to the above

_____

Parent(s) sign here

I understand that my parent(s) has agreed to these rules and agree to help my parent(s) explore the Internet with me.

_____

Child sign here

©2000 SafeKids.Com

Another example of a safety pledge comes from America Online (AOL):

TEN TIPS TO HELP YOU PROTECT YOUR PRIVACY AND SECURITY ONLINE

You can take the responsibility to protect your personal privacy online. Here is a checklist that will help safeguard your privacy and protect the integrity of your computer and AOL account. We urge you to print these tips and post them near your computer for you and your children.

_____ (1) Never give your password to anyone online. Never give your billing information except to facilitate a purchase.

_____ (2) Make your password at least 6 characters in length. Create a password that includes a combination of numbers and letters (such as sun698ray or bell34jar2 or 12hat93). Be sure to use different passwords for each screen name on your account.

_____ (3) If you have fallen for an online scam and gave out your password, change your password right away. Before you sign off, go to Keyword: Password and create a new password for your screen name. Also, change the passwords for any other screen names on your account.

_____ (4) Setting up a Member Profile about yourself can be a good way of connecting with communities of AOL members. But be aware that Member Profiles are public. It's a good idea to avoid including information that could allow people to find you offline, such as your phone number or exact street address.

_____ (5) Use AOL's Mail Controls™ to control the e-mail you and your children receive. You can block e-mail from the Internet, entire domain names and specific e-mail addresses. You can even block the exchange of attached files or pictures in e-mail.

_____ (6) Your computer cannot catch a virus from your opening a piece of e-mail. But if it asks for a password or billing information, or contains a file attachment from someone you don't know, go to Keyword: Notify AOL to learn how to report it.

_____ (7) Never download files unless you know what they are and who sent them to you. Computer viruses and destructive programs that could cause your computer to divulge personal information are often transferred in cleverly disguised files.

_____ (8) When you leave the AOL environment to go on the Web, you may want to check the sites you visit to see if they have a privacy policy. Take special care to protect your personal information and your screen name, since the operators of Web sites are not bound by AOL's privacy policy.

_____ (9) Explain to your children that some non-AOL contests could ask them for personal information, and make very clear what information they may or may not provide, under any circumstances.

_____ (10) You can get instructions to report any violation by going to Keyword: Notify AOL. You can get answers to common questions, and more tips for protecting yourself online, by going to Keyword: Neighborhood Watch.

Copyright © 2001 America Online, Inc. All rights reserved.

As far as my experience with Noah and the problematic Hangman chatter, I decided to calm down. For one, he didn't seem to be bothered by it, and, two, bringing extra attention to it probably would have made him take more note of it. And it gave me a new incentive to spend more time with Noah when he went online, a thought that inspired some of our adventures in the book.

Look to the Cookie

Cookies are bits of information collected by your browser and stored on your hard disk that mark where you've been on the Web. Any personal information—name, address, or what book you bought on Amazon.com—can be retained by a cookie and called up when you return to that site.

Cookies make it possible for sites to personalize information (Hi Ilene!) when you return to places like My Yahoo! They help online sales or service sites like Gap or Barnes &Noble to recall your prior purchases and, by extension, recommend new products. They also track popular links by demographics.

Advertisers, always wanting to make their ads relevant and fresh, use cookies to target your interests. Have you ever noticed how after you browse a travel site, airline or hotel banners wave before your eyes? That's cookies at work. Cookies also are used to securely store personal data that you share with a site, so you don't need to input it over again on your second visit.

When it comes to kids, cookies provide parents with a history of where your kids have gone online and if they have given out unnecessary (and dangerous) information. Some people have expressed concerns that this tracking system violates users privacy.

For the latest on cookies, chomp over to Cookie Central, at **www.cookiecenter.com**. Don't miss "The Unofficial Cookie FAQ" at **www.cookiecentral.com/faq#1.2** for a discussion on disabling and tracing cookies and why these strings of data are called cookies. (See more on cookies and blocking them in Chapter 9, Selling It!)

Filtering
The Internet

Chapter 11

Filtering the Internet

Controversy surrounds the issue of Internet content filtering. While some groups, including the American Library Association, see filtering as a threat to free speech rights, other groups, including many religious organizations, view content filtering as the only way to protect children from viewing inappropriate material online.

What's not at issue is that, given the vast freedom of the Internet, there are many sites that are clearly inappropriate for kids. Although sexual content is most often cited, other material of a graphic, violent, bigoted, hateful, or racist nature also can pop up on a child's screen.

And, unlike other media, the Internet doesn't really offer a good method to separate such materials based on content. As Harry Hochheiser, a board member of the Computer Professionals for Social Responsibility and the author of a FAQ on Internet filtering systems, notes, while you can put a pornographic magazine behind a protective cover, but such material might appear anywhere on the Web. (See the CPSR FAQ at **http://www.cpsr.org/filters/faq.html**.)

"Filters and ratings systems are seen as tools that would provide the cyber-space equivalent of the physical separations that are used to limit access to 'adult material'," says Hochheiser. By preventing access, "The software acts as an auto-mated version of the convenience store clerk who refuses to sell adult-magazines to high-school students."

While no one denies the problem, the question remains: are content filters the solution?

So far, according to Hochheiser and others, the answer has to be a qualified no.

Part of this is the nature of the Net itself. With new sites coming online every hour, it's impossible for every site to be filtered or even rated. Although better blocking systems are becoming available all the time, at present no system has the capability to filter every incoming site on the Web. New Filtered Internet Service Providers claim to screen every site before it comes online. And there are newer attempts to scan information at the modem level.

But even as these systems are implemented, other new technologies, such as peer-to-peer networks that bypass centralized Internet Service Providers make it harder to block problematic sites. Not to mention that many technologically gifted teens quickly figure out how to disable the systems.

Internet Content Filters

Content filters are one or more pieces of software that work together to block kids from viewing offensive online sites.

Most are composed of two components: a ratings system that evaluates sites and filtering software that examines the rating. They can either be 'stand-alone' systems that include both filter software and a list of sites to be blocked (allowed vs. disallowed) or 'protocol-based' systems that first evaluate and rate sites, then filter them.

Whether it's a stand-alone or protocol based system, however, once installed, the effect is the same. Every time you or your child requests information, the protective software examines the site selected. If it's on the "not allowed" list, or doesn't fit the proper PICS rating, then the user will be informed that access is denied. The browser will then block viewing of those pages.

Stand Alone Systems: List Based Ratings

List based systems simply block sites up or down, based on acceptable or unacceptable content.

Who decides what is acceptable? For many vendors, that information remains a 'trade secret.' Most refuse to reveal their lists, or even their criteria for excluding certain sites. Information given on why a particular site is 'disallowed' is often vague and incomplete.

According to Hochheiser, several of these vendors have blocked political sites and sites that criticize blocking software on censorship grounds. Blocked sites have included 'peacefire,' an organization against Internet filtering, and the site of the National Organization of Women.

One variation to list blocking is keyword blocking. Searchers scan sites for objectionable words or phrases and then decide whether or not to block the pages. Two difficulties with keyword searches include a lack of context and an inability to rate graphics on the site. While most software no longer mistakenly block sites for 'breast cancer' or 'chicken breast recipes,' a recent *New York Times* article said that context issues still arise around blocking. For example, a Spanish language health site on diabetes contained the word 'hora' or hour, but because the word also means 'whore' in Swedish, the site might be blocked. In addition, because the blockers don't have graphic capabilities, a sexually explicit or violent photo will be blocked only if the site contains offensive text.

Protocol-Based Systems: Evaluative Ratings

The Platform for Internet Content Selection (PICS) is a protocol for defining ratings, not unlike the MPAA Motion picture ratings. Software that supports PICS can retrieve ratings from sites that rate Web content or from centralized "label bureaus." If ratings don't match the parameters chosen by the software user, then access to the site is denied.

Conceived by the same group that originally rated video games, Internet ratings categorize Web sites based on their content. Vendors like SafeSurf and the Internet Rating Council of America (formerly the Recreational Software Advisory Council (RSCA), which rates video games), evaluate site content based on areas such as 'age range,' 'profanity,' 'heterosexual themes,' 'intolerance,' 'homosexual themes,' 'nudity,' 'violence,' 'sex,' etc.

Once these broad categories are noted, other distinctions may be made. For example, a category like 'nudity' could be configured by a parent to block 'none,' 'partial,' or 'total' nudity.

Anyone can create a ratings system or use the PICS system. The success of such programs, however, depends on two factors: one, how well parents or administrators configure browsers to accept or reject ratings; and two, the willingness of Web page owners to rate their sites accurately, honestly, or at all.

At present, there are but a handful of rating systems in place. And, to judge from the small number of Web pages that have adopted ratings, Hochheiser sees little enthusiasm for the program.

Filtered Internet Service Providers

In response to the shortcomings of selective filtering and parents who want an Internet free from pornography and other inappropriate materials, Filtered Internet Service Providers (ISPs) began to emerge three years ago. At present, there are about two dozen filtered ISPs in the U.S., according to a report from the Center for Democracy and Technology, which conducted a survey of ventures who offer Internet control tools for parents.

Filtered ISPs are sponsored by a variety of groups, including a number of religious organizations, as a way of providing a 'safe' way for children and families to search the Web. All block offensive sites, which can include sites with 'tasteless humor or models wearing lingerie.' Advocates of the service find them more effective than content filters, since they are less likely to be challenged by technologically clever kids.

Some of the same criticisms leveled at content filters have been directed at the filtered ISPs: that they can miss blocking bad sites while banning those that are arguably acceptable. Objectors also protest that these ISPs represent high-tech censorship.

Kids Content Filters and ISPs

Several sites offer comprehensive descriptions of content filters, filtered Internet Service Providers, and other ways parents can monitor content on the Web. Check out:

World Village: Parental Controls ....**www.worldvillage.com/family/parental.html**
Internet Filter Software Chart ....**www.safekids.com/filters.htm**
Internet Content Rating Association ....**www.rsac.org**
SafeSurf ....**www.safesurf.com**
GetNetWise Tools for Families...**www.getnetwise.org**

Issues

Given that there are areas you want your kids to explore, content filters may be the answer for your family. But what if you don't want an outside filter to block sites before you have a chance to evaluate them yourself? Do filters block the very diversity and excitement of discovery of the Web? And what about the generations of thirteen-year-old boys—and some girls—who stole peeks at *Playboy* or *Penthouse* magazines? Is the Internet really that damaging to young minds?

As much as you can, make sure that the sites blocked by your filter match with your beliefs and values. For example, a filter that blocks the keyword 'sex' may also block 'sex education.' Other blocked sites have included feminist sites, gay and lesbian information sites, health sites, and religious sites—often more political than pornographic.

Once again, this is a question only you, as a parent, can answer. For some parents, the interactive nature of the Web makes it a more dangerous commodity. For others, the answer lies in monitoring their kids' Internet use, teaching kids to tell you where they're going, and to report on any disturbing material they might cross online.

So what if you're a concerned parent, but you aren't ready to filter? Here are some recommendations:

→ **Don't panic.** Take comfort: out of the hundreds of thousands of available Web pages, a very small percentage contain objectionable materials. How likely is it that your children might stumble on these sites? And if they do, is it worse than what they might see on cable television?

→ **Get involved.** "Filters don't do a very good job," says Steven Jones, Ph.D, "and kids can often get around them. In many cases the best filter is having a parent who knows the technology and who is willing to take an ongoing role in their children's use of the Internet."

A recent study by Jupiter Research shows that seven out of ten parents prefer watching their kids online rather than putting in filters; the same study showed that six percent used stand alone filtering software. As I've recommended throughout the book, staying in touch with your child's activities—online and off-line—may be an equally good method of keeping them away from troublesome areas of the Net. Talk to your kids about where they go online, in the same way you want to know where they are after school. Draw up a family policy about Internet use that specifies that kids need to tell you if they hit objectionable material online.

→ **Help kids develop critical thinking skills.** Talk to your kids about what is online, and teach them how to look at and evaluate not only the Internet, but all media. Show them how to use a search engine and discuss results. Set up projects before they go online, and then let them report to you afterwards about their experiences.

→ **Offer help.** Set your child's home page to creative educational pages that link to appropriate sites. The American Library Association has gathered Cool Sites for Kids, **www.ala.alsc/children.links.html**. MaMaMedia's search engine presents an 'edited' Web search with sites specifically selected to be fun and child friendly.

→ **Keep the computer in the open.** If you have concerns about how your kids are using the Net, put the computer in a public area—a kitchen alcove, a family room area—where you can keep an eye on online activities.

A list of Content-Filters

Projects: Filters and Kids

→ Have a family filter discussion. Whether or not you decide to filter your Internet connection, talking about what a filter is, how it works, and issues surrounding limiting Internet content are things that make good dinner table discussion, particularly with teens and pre-teens. Some questions: How is the Internet different from other media like TV or magazines? What makes it different? How would your kids feel if someone clipped out offensive articles in a newspaper or magazine? Who should decide what's offensive? Chances are good the conversation might stretch into the next day's meal.

Research the Issues

The Web may be the best place to explore issues around Internet Content Filtering.

For a pro-filtering site, go to Enough is Enough, **www.enough.org**.

The American Library Association has issued a clear explanation of why it believes parents should monitor kids online at libraries, rather than depend on a public institution to censor free speech online. See "Statement on Library Use of Filtering Software", **www.ala.org/alaorg/oif/filt_stm.html**.

Peacefire protests against content filtering on constitutional and privacy grounds. See **www.peacefire.org**.

FamilyClick.com offers a free download of filtering services. Go to **www.familyclick.com**.

What's Next?

Chapter 12

What's Next?

Herewith, a sample of some visions of where the Net, and kids on the Net, are headed. The exciting thing about new technology is not really knowing the future: think of film. It took years before people realized how you could use the medium and to develop new technologies around it to further its use. The same is certainly true of the Internet. Still, here are some folks willing to give their predictions:

"A friend made the observation a few years ago that the Internet makes geography irrelevant. I think his statement was overblown, but in essence he was right. In the future, where you are will matter less and less. People in the remote wilderness of Northern Canada will have access to great art and science, even though they do not live near the Met or the Exploratorium. The Internet will give them the virtual experience of those places."

Jon Katz
Writer
Slashdot.com

"The current vision of the Internet is largely a medium for shopping. The most important change over the next five years is that it will become a medium for content. Buying online by that time will become as ordinary as the local Kids-R-Us. The new thing will be accessing rich, attractively presented and extremely useful information."

Michael Antecol
Wired Youth Analyst
Forrester Research, Inc.

"I look forward to the Massachusetts Institute of Technology initiative to have every class available online and hope other universities follow suit. I think there are obvious advantages to face-to-face learning, but for kids who don't have that option—because of money, because of geography, I think this is a whole lot better than nothing.

"I'd like Rakaya, my daughter, to participate in an online Great Books program when she's in high school. There are already several of these operating, but right now they're all Christian and we're not, so we'll wait and see. In the meantime, we use the Internet for research, for fun, for communication, and in my case, work. She sees the adults in the home using it and naturally wants to be part of it, and I think that's the real message here: kids use of any technology which will parallel adults' prioritization of it and the manner in which we use it ourselves.

"That's where our responsibility begins."

Linda Fokkena
Communications Director
KITE
www.kiteinc.org

"Parents will realize that learning about technology and how they can help their kids use it is a necessary skill. We'll recognize that there isn't one right way or wrong way for kids and families to adapt to technology, but that each family will have to find their own way and fit their own needs.

"In the future, technology will be everywhere in ways we can hardly imagine. In the office, homes, school, everyone will be more surrounded by technology, making us more sophisticated about how we integrate it into our lives.

"More and more, kids will be in the driver's seat when it comes to learning experiences, as they explore technology and learn how to discover what it has to offer. The Net is perfect for open-ended discovery, the sort that makes kids want to learn. Kids will also use the Net to express themselves—by making Web pages, building digital artifacts. Digital media will help them communicate their ideas.

"And then, maybe most exciting, they'll get to exchange those ideas. Kids learn by doing, and by exchanging information and ideas, online kids will become active, not passive, learners . They'll collaborate and share. They can put up Web pages at MamaMedia so everyone can see them—sort of a global refrigerator where kids can post their artwork!

"The most important issue is balance. New technologies will give kids power. They'll be toolboxes for new types of learning and understanding."

Idit Harel
President and founder
www.MaMaMedia.com

"Filtering content on the Internet to make it safe for kids is not that easy. Blocking software, at least what's on the market right now, isn't a total answer to content problems: kids can get around it, and the Internet is too big to control completely.

"What parents will figure out—if they haven't already—is that the Internet isn't the end of the world. People thought that of rock and roll, and so far Western Civilization hasn't gone under. I think that as parents spend more time with kids online, they'll realize that the Internet is simply part of the culture that they'll learn to deal with in a reasonable way. Because while content filters and blocking software will get better technically, it's not like in six months we'll have the problem solved."

Harry Hochheiser
Board Member, CPSR (Computer Professionals for Social Responsibility)

"I think what the Internet offers is a choice, another alternative for teachers and students to improve the classroom. But for the Internet to be useful for students, I think it has to be made somewhat less chaotic; the current bandwidth will have to increase to improve multimedia possibilities. Yet I expect that someday soon, with technical improvements, kids will have a choice between virtual learning experiences.

"For teachers, the Internet means change. For those who learned to teach in one way, the Internet has the possibility to change the dynamic and how a teacher interfaces with the material. Where teachers once 'owned' the material and told kids how to use it and what it 'meant,' now they'll be challenged to share information in new ways and to become "collaborators" with kids in the learning process. I see more social interaction when it comes to learning."

Catherine Schifter, Ph.D
Temple University
Associate Professor
Department of Curriculum, Instruction & Technology in Education

"People will think seriously about the goals of using technology in the classroom and how to evaluate it. Teachers will be like travel agents—you tell them where you want to go and they'll advise you on your excursion needs—they'll find out what you need to know and where you want to go, then use their knowledge, experience, and wisdom to offer advice, evaluation, and assessment. Teachers will give kids goals and purpose when they use technology.

"Classrooms will change. Kids won't be in one grade, but in multi-year grades, so they can develop relationships with several teachers and work in teams with kids of different ages.

"Teachers will have tech teaching certificates as more school boards realize what they need to stay up to date. The emphasis won't be on producing knowledge, but on creative problem solving, tenacity, and open-ended problem solving. Computers are incredibly flexible, and they'll bring a new open-ended sense of exploration with them."

Kyle Peck, Ph.D
Penn State University
Professor, Education and Technology

"A recent study I completed showed that while computer video games resulted in behavior problems for kids, the more time study participants spent on the Internet, the better their behavior became. In other words, for that study, the Internet appears to be a positive influence.

"My hope for the future? If parents want their kids to spend time online, they need to make sure of the content, and they need to take control of the kids' time on the Web. Get to know the technology and spend time with your kids online."

Larry Rosen, Ph.D
California State University
Professor, Psychology
www.technostress.com

"There seems to be no question that the Internet is the future of computing. In this future, software will increasingly reside on remote servers that you access through the Internet, not in your personal computer.

"In around five years, for example, most teenagers will stop buying music on CDs. Instead they will purchase subscriptions to web sites that will house vast libraries of music and allow them to download a set number of tracks that will remain functional for a set period of time, say three months. The solution will make everyone happy. The consumers will have a lot more current music than they ever had in the past, and won't mind if the license expires quickly (because you get sick of the music anyway after a while). And the music companies will be happy about the much larger volume of sales they will have.

"Little kids' CD-ROMs will go the same way. The market will dry up for products such as JumpStart and Reader Rabbit. Instead people will buy subscriptions to Web sites that update every week or two—cleverisland.com is a good example of this that currently exists on the Internet."

Laurence Miller, Ph.D
Director of Education
Alfy, Inc.

"I think the next generation will be—and already is—much more comfortable with technology than their parents. They will have less anxiety and fear about it. They will be savvier about assessing the validity of information, and will be more sophisticated in understanding the nuances of 'reality' and 'fantasy.' While we all may go through a phase of idealizing and becoming overly involved in the Internet, the end result will be that future generations will use cyberspace as a springboard for fully appreciating the beauty of the 'real world.'

"But then I'm an optimist."

Jon Suler, Ph.D
Rider College
Associate Professor, Psychology

"Within the next twenty years, there is very little that I do not expect to happen for the Internet. I have seen so many phenomenal sites over the past five years and so much technical improvement occur that my personal optimism about the future of the Internet can't be overestimated. Specifically, I can imagine the Web merging all kinds of media telephone, radio, television, movies and literature—into one huge communication center. I know this scares a lot of people but I think it would be cool."

Sasha Rush
Junior, Cheltenham High School

"The Internet is great. It can only get greater."

Noah Rush
Fourth Grader, Wyncote Elementary School

Glossary

Applet

A small computer program designed to do a specific job. Applets are often built into Web pages to run animations or programs such as 'chat.'

ARPANET

The Advanced Research Project Agency Network (ARPANET) began in the late 1960s as scientists started to connect university and government computers. Scientists and researchers needed to exchange data and electronic mail, while Defense Department officials wanted to use the new networked computers to communicate if a nuclear war caused conventional communications technologies to collapse. ARPANET formed the basis for the modern Internet.

Banner

An advertisement that crosses a Web page.

Blocking Software

Software and rating systems designed to filter objectionable online content. Filters often block pornographic, violent, bigoted, or hate-filled sites, with an aim to protecting children from viewing such information. Corporations may also use this software to block such information from employees.

Boolean

A common system of logic developed by mathematician George Boole based on operators such as AND, OR, and NOT that is commonly used by search engines.

Browser

As the doorway to the Web, browsers fetch Web pages. But modern browsers are also configured to run audio and visual programs; secure e-commerce transactions; run Java applets; filter Internet sites based on ratings systems, as well as other sophisticated uses. The two most popular browser programs are Microsoft Internet Explorer and Netscape Navigator.

Bulletin Boards (Discussion Boards)

A computer system used to post electronic messages, store files, and run discussions. Most bulletin boards are focused on a specific topic.

Chat

Real time discussion online, chat is one of the most popular uses of the Net. Chat can take a number of forms, from open discussion rooms of Internet Relay Chat (IRC) to one-on-one of Instant Messaging (IM) and ICQ.

Cookie

A cookie is a string of information that a Web site sends to your hard disk each time you visit the site. Cookies can personalize information, aid with online sales, or track demographics or popular links. Cookies are commonly used to rotate and customize banner ads based on information you've provided the Web sites.

Demos

1) A sample download of a commercial product that you can buy in a store, a demo is usually a "taste" of the real software, often a game. 2) Brief multimedia projects featuring animation, sound, and music created by programmers to 'demonstrate' their ability.

Domain

The name of a site on the Internet. For example, www.thebestsite.com is the domain name for a specific address on the Internet called thebestsite.com. The ".com" part is the top-level domain, while "thebestsite" is the second-level domain.

Download

To request and receive a file from another computer on the Internet.

E-Mail

Electronic messages sent from one computer to another.

Emoticon

Emoticons or "smilies" replace visual and auditory cues in regular one-on-one conversation.

FAQ

A list of "Frequently Asked Questions" (FAQ), about a website, topic, service, or product. FAQs are found throughout the Web, explaining just about everything.

Flame

An abusive or angry communication sent via e-mail, on chat, or other communication areas of the Web. Flames and flamewars can be sparked by a lack of proper netiquette.

404 Not Found

Generally annoying page indicating that the Web site you're seeking is connected to a bad link, is un-available, is down, or never existed at all. Double check the address, or try to locate the site or resource using your favorite search engine.

FTP

File Transfer Protocol is the standard that governs how computers exchange files over the Internet.

Freeware

Programming that is available at no cost to you. To access freeware, you simply need to download it. You need to remember, however, that most freeware is is still copyrighted, which means you can't use it or copy it into your own programming.

Game Modifications

Game modifications ("mods") are extensions or variations of familiar computer games. This add-on software to pre-existing games is designed and developed for sole release on the Net. Mod designers are often fans of a certain game, who might want to extend the life of a game.

Hardware

A term for the nuts, bolts, and wires of computer equipment and the actual computer and related machines.

Hit

The term for information that results from a Web search. A "hit" is when the computer finds a possible answer (Web site) to a search inquiry, e.g., my search for information about the group "Phish" generated a million, four thousand "hits." Hits can also refer to the number of times people view a particular Web page.

Home Page

For Web sites, the home page serves as the doorway for all other pages. Often, these pages contain navigation information on how to get around the rest of the site. For Internet users, the home page is the first page they see when they connect to the Web, often the home page of the browser, though users acan choose any Web Page as their browser home page.

HTTP

The Hypertext Transfer Protocol is the standard used by World Wide Web servers to move text, graphic images, sound, video, and other files across the Internet.

HTML

Hypertext Markup Language is a collection of symbols or codes that tells your Web browser how to display a Web pages' words and images. Each individual markup code is referred to as an "element" or "tag."

Icon

This is a small picture on a Web page that represents the topic or information category on another Web page. An icon is often the hypertext link to that page.

ICQ

ICQ ("I Seek You") is a one-on-one chat program similar to AOL's IM (Instant Messenger) and MSN Messenger that allows users to carry on conversations over the Internet. Both parties must download the same IM software to participate in the conversation and be online at the same time.

Image File

Image files are pictures stored in electronic form on the World Wide Web in compressed form, to shorten their downloading time. Files are stored under formulas that can be understood by Web browsers: ".gif" or ".jpeg" or ".png."

Internet

A global collection of computer networks that permits people to find and use information and communicate with others.

ISP

An Internet Service Provider (ISP) is any company that can connect you to the Internet, provide e-mail boxes, design and host Web pages, help secure domain names, or other Internet related services.

Link

A link is a connection between pages or images on the Web. Links often appear as underlined words or phrases, highlighted text, or images. By clicking onto the text or image, users are transferred to a new location.

Listserv

A listserver program distributes e-mail to everyone include on a e-mail list, usually topic specific. Users subscribe to the list and will then receive mail sent to everyone on that list. Most lists allow subscribers to send messages of their own to the listserv, and thus to every other subscriber.

Lurk

Term for observing, as a non-participant, Internet features such as chat, games, etc. Lurkers often stay 'invisible' until they learn the rules, then join in.

MMOGs

Massively Multiplayer Online Games (MMOGs). These games have no single player component, and are played entirely online. Players experience the game with hundreds or even thousands of others playing at the same time.

Modem

A device that allows computers to communicate with each other over telephone lines by changing digital signals to telephone signals for transmission and then back to digital signals. Modems come in different speeds: the higher the speed, the faster the data is transmitted.

MOO

A Multi-user Object-Oriented (MOO) environment allows participants to travel a virtual environment and interact in real time. A descendant of MUDs (Multi-user Domain) which were often used for gaming, MOOs have assumed a variety of uses, including educational ones.

MP3

MP3 is a data compression format that records and compresses music files into packages small enough to be efficiently transfered over the Internet, while maintaining near CD sound quality.

Netiquette

An informal set of rules or good manners that govern polite interactions online.

Newbie

Newcomers to the Net experience. You know who you are.

Online Service

Companies such as American Online or Prodigy that provide members access to the Internet through their own special user interface as well as providing additional services such as chat rooms, children's areas, travel planning, and financial management.

Password

Phrase or combination of letters or numbers required to register with or enter certain protected sites.

Peer-to-Peer

A decentralized way of exchanging files, often accomplished 'under the radar' of the user's Internet Service Provider. Originally popularized by the Napster music service as a way to trade music between users, peer-to-peer Napster 'clones' now can be found across the Web.

PICS

The Platform for Internet Content Selection (PICS) is a protocol for defining ratings, not unlike the MPAA Motion picture ratings. Software that supports PICS can retrieve ratings from sites that rate Web content or from centralized "label bureaus." If ratings don't match the parameters chosen by the software user, access to the site is denied.

Pop/Pop 3 (Post Office Protocol)

This is a mail protocol used to service intermittent dial-up connections to the Internet. Mail is held until you access the account, when it gets transferred to your computer.

Portal

The name for the home site or major gateway for users when they first enter the Web. This might be a Web browser page, or a site you select.

Postcardware

This no-charge software that is freely shared with one caveat: users are required to send the software provider a postcard as a form of payment. The idea is to humanize the transaction, reminding the user that someone else shared something freely and telling the provider that someone is actually using the creation.

Protocol

A set of rules composed to determine how computers interact with one another.

Plug-In

A small piece of software that extends the capabilities of a larger program. Internet browsers rely on plug-ins to play audio and video files, for example.

Search Engine

Program designed to find, collect, and retrieve information about Web sites from Web sites. Users can then search through this collected information to help them find Web sites of interest.

Shareware

Shareware is software distributed on a trial basis on the honor system. If you use it regularly, you're required to eventually register and pay for it. When you pay, you usually get additional technical assistance or upgrades on the material.

Some software developers offer a shareware version of programs with a built-in expiration date. (After 30 days or 20 uses, for example, the user can no longer get access to the program) Shareware can also be offered with certain capabilities disabled as an enticement to buy the complete version of the program.

SMTP (Simple Mail Transfer Protocol)

The most common protocol used for transferring e-mail across the Internet.

Spam

Unsolicited e-mail.

Software

A computer program or set of instructions for your computer. System software operates on the machine itself and is invisible to you. Application software lets you carry out certain activities, such as word processing and games.

Tag

Each individual markup code in HTML is referred to as an "element" or "tag."

TCP/IP

Transmission Control Protocol (TCP) is software that manages the transfer of data across networks. TCP bundles information into packets, while IP delivers the packets to the right location.

WebCam

Camera attached to the Web that broadcasts live pictures in real time. WebCams have taken pictures of street corners, mountain tops, and – our personal favorite – a really cute hamster taking part in a study on natural body rhythms.

W3C

The World Wide Web Consortium (W3C) sets protocols and provides helpful facts on every area of Web operations.

Webmaster

The person, or persons, who design, update, and maintain the operation of a Web site.

URL

The Uniform Resource Locator (URL) is the World Wide Web address of a site on the Internet.

Introduction

http://pbskids.org. /did_you_know/license

This PBS web site offers a test to get your "Internet license" along with games based on familiar television shows.

Chapter One: What is the Internet, Anyway?

www.isoc.org/internet

The Internet SOCiety is a professional society with more than 150 organizational and 6,000 individual members in over 100 countries that addresses issues involving the future of the Internet. Contains a number of links on the operation and history of the Net.

www.pbs.org/opb/nerds2.0.1

An interesting site based on PBS program "Nerds 2.0.1" which profiles some players in the development of the computer industry.

www.ideafinder.com

A good place to start learning about great Idea Finders like Tim Berners-Lee, 'inventor' of the Web.

www.w3.org

The site of the World Wide Web Consortium. An organization designed to promote the full potential of the Web, the group – headed by Tim Berners-Lee develops interoperable technologies including guidelines, specifications, software and tools for the Web.

http://web.mit.edu/invent/index.html

Site of Invention Dimension, the MIT site that celebrates the inventive spirit.

www.privateline.com/TelephoneHistory/History1.htm

A history of telecommunications presented by Tom Farley.

www.inventorsmuseum.com/television.htm

The history of inventions from A-Z. Lots of fun images and factoids.

www.thelist.com or www.thedirectory.org

Find an Internet Service Provider.

Chapter Two: Searching the World Wide Web

www.encyclopedia.com
The Encyclopedia online.

www.encarta.com
Reference online.

www.britannica.com
Britannica online.

www.kidsclick.org
Web search for kids organized by librarians

www.yahooligans.com
Kids' directory from Yahoo!

www.awesomelibrary.com
Awesome Library, a kids' directory, organizes the Web with 17,000 carefully reviewed resources.

www.mamamedia.com
Children's site filled with innovative interactive games, unusual search engines and kids'clubs. The site offers a place for kids to connect with one another and post creative original work.

http://score.rims.k12.ca.us/activity/LBSite
The Luther Burbank Virtual Museum

www.madsci.org
The MadSci Network is the "collective cranium of scientists providing answers to kids (and adults)questions along with a variety of oddities and other ends as well". A fun and informative site.

http://micro.magnet.fsu.edu/primer/java/scienceopticsu
Science, Optics and You present Java applets that dramatically illustrate the effects of scale and size in the nature and the universe.

www.travlang.com/languages
Travlang's Foreign Languages for Travellers offers Afrikaans to Zulu with many, many choices in between.

www.altavista.com
Alta Vista search site.

www.go.com
Go search site.

www.google.com
Google search site, one of the best.

www.hotbot.lycos.com
HotBot search site.

www.northernlight.com
Northern Light search site.

www.planetsearch.com
Planet Search meta search engine.

www.yahoo.com
Yahoo! Web directory.

www.excite.com
Excite Web directory.

www.dmoz.com
Dmoz – the Open Directory Project.

www.lii.org
Librarians Index to the Internet, Web resource directory of sources evaluated by librarians for librarians and non-librarians.

www.looksmart.com
LookSmart Web directory.

www.search.com
CNET Web meta search.

www.dogpile.com
Dogpile Web meta search engine. One of the best.

www.ithaki.net/kids or http://www.todalanet.com/kids
A metasearch Web engine of kids' sites. One of the best.

www.metacrawler.com
   Metacrawler meta search engine.

www.momma.com
   Momma meta search engine.

www.profusion.com
   Profusion meta search engine.

www.searchenginewatch.com
   Everything you ever wanted to know about search engines can be found at
Search Engine Watch. Sign up for their daily e-bulletins on the latest search tips
and search news.

Chapter Three: Sending E-Mail

http://my.email.address.is/index.htm
   My E-mail Address Is helps locate elusive e-mail addresses. Could life be any
simpler? (Also try http://people.yahoo.com www.switchboard.com/,
www.whowhere.lycos.com/, www.infospace.com/, and www.iaf.net/)

www.kidscom.com
   KidsCom site for kids to connect via home pages, chat and e-mail.

www.ks-connection.org
   Kids Space Connection is a monitored site for kids to connect via e-mail and
bulletin boards.

www.cyberkids.com
   Cyberkids tries to provide a voice for kids on the Internet by publishing creative work by kids ages 7-12 and to help kids connect in chat rooms and message
boards. They also have a Cyberteens site for older kids..

www.topica.com
   Topica offers hundreds of listservs, newsletters and discussion groups.

http://catalog.com/vivian/interest-group-search.html
   Excellent site for listservs.

www.kidlink.org
   Kidlink provides IRC chat connections for kids around the world.

www.wsu.edu/DrUniverse/Contents.html
So why don't spiders stick to their own webs? Ask Dr. Universe, a know-it-all who knows-it all.

www.hotmail.com
Popular site to get a free e-mail connection. Also fetch one at www.juno.com, www.email.com/, www.prontomail.com/prontomail/login/login.asp, or http://mail.yahoo.com/.

http://postcards.www.media.edu/Postcards/cardrack.html
Find interesting postcards to e-mail at the Postcards cardrack.

www.bluemountain.com
Blue Mountain Cards offers a wide selection of musical animated cards for every occasion.

www.e-cards.com
E-cards that generate benefits to the environment with every click of the mouse can be send at this ecologically friendly site.

Chapter Four: IRC, Chat and Discussion Boards

www.irchelp.org
The most complete IRC help site online with a thousand helpful files including FAQs, primers, guides and downloadable clients to run IRC on your computer. Highly recommended.

Chapter Five: Build Your Own Web Page

http://www.w3.org/MarkUp/Guide
Dave Raggett's short introduction to writing HTML.

www.excite.com/info/getting_listed/meta_tags
A short and sweet Meta Description of how to get your site listed onto a search engine using meta tags, courtesy of Excite.

www.dynamicdrive.com/dynamicindex4/flyimage.htm
How to put floating images on your Web page, from the good people at Dynamic Drive.

www.w3.org/People/Raggett/tidy

A nifty piece of software that will clean up your HTML from Dave Raggett. It's a bit technical, but worth looking at.

http://validator.w3.org

This Validator software checks to see if your HTML meets the specifications of the W3Consortium, which sets the standards for the World Wide Web.

www.homestead.com

Homestead is an excellent place to host your website. Check out recently instituted fee schedule. For free sites, try Geocities.Yahoo! (http://geocities.yahoo.com) and Angelfire (www.angelfire.com).

www.tucows.com/preview/194531.html

Spot to download a super kids' homepage editor, Hot Dog Jr.

www.greatestplaces.org

Explore some of the seven Greatest Places on Earth on this interactive children's geographic site.

www.buttonmaker.com

Buttons for websites and other clip art to spark your artistic imagination.

http://animfactory.com

Over 15,000 free images at the Animation Factory.

www.kidsdomain.com/clip

Kids' Domain focuses on kids' art and holidays.

http://disneyclipart.com

Mickey and the gang are all here at Disney Clip Art.

http://gallery.yahoo.com

Photos fill the galleries of Yahoo! art. (Check out the baby seals for cute.)

www.coolarchive.com

Sounds, arrows, bullets, buttons, applications are all free and waiting at the Cool Archive.

Chapter Six: Playing around

www.ea.com
Good place to download games.

www.surfnetkids.com
Surf the Net collects online games suitable for the younger and preschool set.

www.games.com
Good selection of traditional board games adapted to the Net.

www.shockwave.com
A favorite game site with preteens and teens alike.

www.neopets.com/addpet.phtml
Drive yourself crazy – adopt a neopet and try to keep it alive.

www.happypuppy.com
Another popular game site.

www.yavsort.com
Paint ball for toddlers.

www.quizsite.com
Diabolical site for pop culture fans.

www.sikids.com/fantasy/baseball
Fantasy sports of all sorts for 8-12 year olds.

www.tennislovers.com/index2.htm?games/onlinegames.htm
Virtual tennis games.

http://games.yahoo.com
Many clever variations on Scrabble.

http://clevermedia.com
Clever Media invites you to make your own game.

www.goobo.com/monster
Make your own monster with Goobo.

www.scholastic.com/ispy/make/index.htm
I Spy on the computer sponsored by publisher Scholastic Books.

www.funbrain.com/brainbowl/twoplay.html
Brain Bowl tests your wits via e-mail with a competitor on academic questions.

www.lizardpoint.com/fun/geoquiz/usaquiz.html
So where is Arkansas? Locate the States in a fast moving map game.

www.solitairenetwork.com
Variations of solitaire, everywhere.

www.msoworld.com/playgames.html
One hundred and six games to be played against other users or bots.

www.mindpixel.com/About/about.php3
Help feed the brain of a developing AI named "GAC" (Jack) by writing "Mindpixels"—unambiguous yes-no statements. Instructions on the site. Intriguing.

www.robocup.org
Humanoid Robot Soccer players anyone? That's the challenge at Robocup, who want to put together a team to defeat we humans by 2050.

www.oozinggoo.com/20q
Old car trip favorite: Twenty Questions.

Chapter Seven: Classroom, Homeschooling and Distance Learning

www.globe.gov/fsl/welcome.html
The GLOBE Program brings together K-12 students, teachers, and scientists from around the world who work together to help learn more about the environment.

http://whale.wheelock.edu/Welcome.html
WhaleNet's interactive educational web site focuses on whales and marine research.

www.epals.com

epals connects over 3.8 million students and teachers in 191 countries.

www.rc.umd.edu/rchs/rchsmoo.htm

The Romantic High School MOO (Multiuser Domain using Object-Oriented programming) dedicated to education in Romantic Period literature. It's occupied by real-life classes and teachers from around the U.S., as well as a library of electronic texts, a teachers' lounge, and shared spaces for special events and social interaction.

www.digitaldivide.gov

Falling Through the Net web site provides information about efforts to provide all Americans with access to the Net and other information and technologies as well as other reports and information on the "digital divide." www.puzzle-maker.com – Make your own puzzle on this innovative site.

http://pixel.cs.vt.edu/melissa/projects.html

A number of Internet projects used in Virginia schools.

www.zen.org/~brendan/kids.html

Kids on the Web site has a number of links to fun kids projects online.

http://ology.amnh.org

OLOGY is the science site for the American Museum of Natural History in New York.

www.starnet.org

Distance learning consortium.

www.laurelsprings.com

Laurel Springs School online education.

Chapter Eight: Teens Online

www.winamp.com

Winamp radio and plug-in center.

www.live-at.com/index.html

LIVE @ offers online chat, radio, and broadcasts.

www.midi.com

MIDI is a musical instrument digital interface that makes it easier to compose original music.

www.envy.nu/antigrrrl/ring

"Oh Just Shut Up…You're Only 16" links a number of teen sites into a 'ring' of connected sites.

www.purplepjs.com

purplepjs is an online 'zine by and for girls.

www.bluejeanmedia.com

A company that encourages young women to create their own media, online and off.

www.gurl.com

gurl.com is an online 'zine for young women. Other zines include www.react.com and www. planetgirl.com/.

www.aol.com/aim/home.html

Home of AOL Instant Messenger (IM). Similar services can be found at http://messenger.msn.com, http://messenger.yahoo.com, www.jabbercentral.com and www.shazmo.com.

www.netbored.com

Netbored Video offers streaming band video of all types. Other sites that provide similar services include www.atomfilms.com, and www.cinemanow.com.

http://tesla.liketelevision.com

Old television anyone? Like Television offers the latest old Johnny Carson, Three Stooges and Bonanza reruns.

www.mightybigtv.com

Mighty Big TV presents reviews more worth reading than the stuff they were watching.

http://espn.go.com

ESPN highlights.

http://expn.go.com

Skateboarders and other extreme sporters, unite.

www.salon.com

Salon provides literate articles and reviews of popular and not-so-popular cultural and political life.

www.slate.com

Another literate e-zine, Slate.

www.pewinternet.org

The Pew Foundation has undertaken to chart the Internet habits of our nation. Follow the results at their online site.

Chapter Nine: Selling It

http://harrypotter.warnerbros.com

Official fan site for the Harry Potter movie.

www.ftc.gov/kidzprivacy

Government site that explains COPPA to kids.

www.candystand.com

Lifesavers Candystand Shockwave game site.

www.britneyspears.com

Official fan site for Britney Spears.

www.cme.org

The Center for Media Education, a watchdog group that works to ensure that the media serves the public interest through research, education and policy efforts. Click to www.cme.org/publications/Singer35.pdf to read "Digital Kids: The New Online Consumer Culture", by Kathryn Montgomery, Center for Media Education, in Adobe PDF format

www.mediachannel.org/atissue/consumingkids/front.shtml

Media Channel offers a thought provoking series of articles from various sources on advertising to kids and its impact.

www.privacyrights.org

How are your children's privacy rights affected online? This site has some answers along with a resource guide for parents.

www.epic.org

The site of the Electronic Privacy Information Center covers the issues surrounding privacy online.

www.junkbusters.com

Junkbusters offers more information than you could possibly use on how to block anything you might not want online, including popup ads or spam.

Chapter Ten: Protecting Your Kids Online

**www.safekids.com, www.safeteens.com,
www.safekids.com/filters.htm**

Safekids.com, an organization devoted to child and teen safety online, provides a comprehensive listing of all Internet filters and blocking services. Recommended.

www.cookiecenter.com

The place to find information about cookies and how they are used online. A complete FAQ on cookies is available on the site, at www.cookiecentral.com/faq#1.2.

Chapter Eleven: Filtering the Internet

www.cpsr.org/filters/faq.html

Computer Professionals for Social Responsibility FAQ on Internet Content Filters. Answers many questions parents may have on the topic in a clear, non-technical way.

www.worldvillage.com/family/parental.html

World Village offers a list of filtering and protective services for families to block offensive Web sites.

www.safesurf.com

Safe Surf offers self-rating tools for Internet sites.

www.getnetwise.org/tools

Get Net Wise offers a tool for determining what type of filter best suits families needs.

www.enough.org

Enough is Enough is a site devoted to stopping illegal pornography and online predators directed towards children and families on the Internet.

www.ala.org/alaorg/oif/filt_stm.html

Statement of Library Use on Filtering Software in which the American Library Association asserts that the rights of free speech overrule any need to filter the Internet in public library settings.

www.peacefire.org

Peacefire opposes all Internet filtering on grounds that it interferes with Constitutionally protected rights of free speech.

www.familyclick.com

Family Click, a family friendly Internet Filtered Service Provider.

Domains

A

B

C

D

E

F

Kids' Pledge

I will not give out personal information such as my address, telephone number, parents' work address/telephone number, or the name and location of my school without my parents' permission.

I will tell my parents right away if I come across any information that makes me feel uncomfortable.

I will never agree to get together with someone I 'meet' online without first checking with my parents. If my parents agree to the meeting, I will be sure that it is in a public place and bring my mother or father along.

I will never send a person my picture or anything else without first checking with my parents.

I will not respond to any messages that are mean or in any way make me feel uncomfortable. It is not my fault if I get a message like that. If I do, I will tell my parents right away so that they can contact the service provider.

I will talk with my parents so that we can set up rules for going online. We will decide upon the time of day that I can be online, the length of time I can be online, and appropriate areas for me to visit. I will not access other areas or break these rules without their permission

I will not give out my Internet password to anyone (even my best friends), other than my parents.

I will be a good online citizen and not do anything that hurts other people or is against the law.

I agree to the above

_____

Child sign here

I will help my child follow this agreement and will allow reasonable use of the Internet as long as these rules and other family rules are followed.

_____

Parent(s) sign here

Parents' Pledge

I will get to know the services and Web.

I will set reasonable rules and guidelines for computer use by my children and will discuss these rules and post them near the computer as a reminder.

I'll remember to monitor their compliance with these rules, especially when it comes to the amount of time they spend on the computer and/or Web sites. If I don't know how to use them, I'll get my child to show me how.

I will not overreact if my child tells me about a problem he or she is having on the Internet. Instead, we'll work together to try to solve the problem and prevent it from happening again.

I promise not to use a PC or the Internet as an electronic babysitter.

I will help make the Internet a family activity and ask my child to help plan family events using the Internet.

I will try get to know my child's "online friends" just as I try get to know his or her other friends.

I agree to the above

_____

Parent(s) sign here

I understand that my parent(s) has agreed to these rules and agree to help my parent(s) explore the Internet with me.

_____

Child sign here

©2000 SafeKids.Com

West Coast or East Coast?
America's greatest cities are waiting.

A Parent's Guide™ to
Los Angeles

ISBN 0-9675127-1-9
UPC 679762060029
$14.95
7.375"x9.125"
192 pages.

A Parent's Guide™ to
New York City

ISBN 0-9675127-0-0
UPC 679762060012
$14.95
7.375"x9.125"
192 pages.

MARS®
PUBLISHING

**6404 Wilshire Blvd
Los Angeles CA 90048**

800-549-6646

www.marspub.com

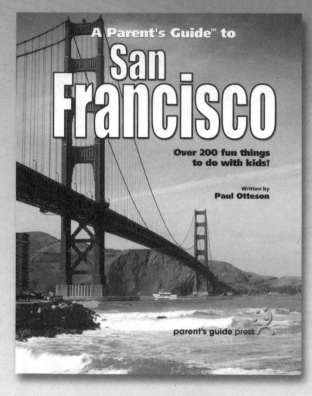
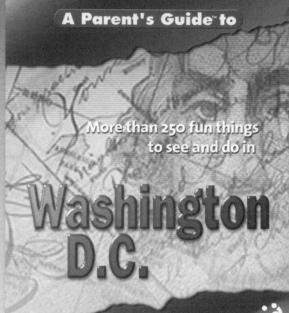